The Hun...

The Universe is a limitless circle with a limitless radius.

The Universe is an infinite gathering of infinitely small particles.

The Universe is constantly moving and changing.

Master Koichi Tohei

These are the fundamental principles of the Universe that we live in. They characterize and govern all objects from the planets to peanuts, all human relationships, and all of man's endeavors from simple movements to complex undertakings. In Aikido, we study these principles to better live in harmony and rhythm with these natural conditions.

Whether you are a seven or eight year old youngster, a seventy or eighty year old senior, or somewhere in between, the principles that define the human experience are the same. These principles are not only a phenomenon or condition of the physical universe, but arise from, and truly reflect, the authentic state of our Original Mind. And this is not something either exotic, religious, or even particularly spiritual, but merely the way of becoming a real human being.

Christopher Curtis

KI-AIKIDO
ON
MAUI

A Training Manual

Written and compiled by
Christopher Curtis

First Edition 1982 Second Edition 1995 Third Edition 2001

Fourth Edition 2019

For additional information write to:

Maui Ki-Aikido
P.O. Box 724
Wailuku, Maui, Hawaii 96793

This is a publication of MAKS Publications

Library of Congress Cataloging-in Publication Data
Curtis, Christopher
Ki-Aikido On Maui: a training manual / by Christopher Curtis —
3rd ed.

p.cm.

ISBN 0-9655021-1-2

1.Aikido 2. Sports 3. Spiritual/Philosophy

Printed in the United States of America

Cover design: Joelle Chicheportiche Perz
Photos: Chris Barense

FIVE PLEDGES OF JISENKAI

1. *Today, I will spend the day with a plus face.*
2. *Today, I will use plus words.*
3. *Today, I will do my activities with plus thinking.*
4. *Today, I will build a plus society.*
5. *Today, I will pray for world peace with a plus mind.*

CONTENTS

FOREWORD TO THE 4TH EDITION

I am honored and grateful to have been asked to write a few introductory words. It is surely not my place to add any further words of praise directed at the Masters described in this book. Each day my heart is filled with gratitude just to have known and have access to the wisdom of the Founder (Soshu), Master Koichi Tohei, and his senior students, Iwao Tamura Sensei (in Japan) and Shinichi Suzuki Sensei (outside Japan).

Christopher Curtis Sensei has been studying personal and spiritual development for over 50 years and he began living at the feet of his teacher, Suzuki Sensei, over four decades ago. His life example as both a student and teacher illustrate, and even embody, a commitment to real training (*shugyo*). Along the way he developed a deep grasp of Ki principles, which is a blessing for another generation of persons seeking to understand the Way of the Universe. We are all very grateful to Curtis Sensei for completing this revised and updated book. With each edition Curtis Sensei "empties his cup" as he shares his insights in clear and simple language.

As with previous editions, this 4th edition is much more than a "Training Manual."

Curtis Sensei's revised explanations of the most important aspects of "committed training" (*shugyo*) and the "inner disciplines" evidence profound insight. I know that Suzuki Sensei experienced much pride and joy as he fully realized (and observed for himself) that he had passed along so much in the lifetime development of his senior student Curtis Sensei. As is written in this book, TIME is our most precious gift, and Suzuki Sensei invested it wisely in the training and development of the author. All students of Ki-Aikido can benefit by keeping a copy of this revised book on hand at all times; in your training bag, at your bedside table, and in your office.

When Curtis Sensei travels to train in Japan each year, he is reminded to "empty his cup" before boarding the plane. And, as evidenced by this revised 4th edition, I know that the author is committed to keeping this manual current. The training described in each successive edition reflects Curtis Sensei's continual discovery of new means of both expanding our awareness and deepening our understanding of the timeless, universal truths that are

always present just waiting to be experienced by anyone
and everyone.

David Shaner,
Chief Instructor Eastern Ki Federation
and HQ Advisor to Eastern Europe/
Russia Ki Federation

INTRODUCTION

When I first began training Aikido many years ago, I had little knowledge of practice in Eastern martial arts, and no experience whatsoever of Aikido. The various forms of Aikido practice, the multitude of requirements for what appeared to be an endless series of tests, and the seemingly vague and (who knew?!) perhaps arbitrary rules of etiquette which everyone except me seemed to be taking for granted, struck me as somewhat intimidating and possibly even insurmountable. Adding to this sense of strangeness, there seemed to be no final consensus, no one seemed to be in agreement as to the exact nature, sequence or even, in some cases, the existence of these various requirements for proper training and personal development.

In the beginning, I found myself, out of an eagerness to learn, (and frankly a desire to "fit in" and not "make waves"), beginning to accept this vagueness as "just the way it is" and proceeded to concentrate on developing the specific skills and attitude adjustments that were required of me on any particular day, and at any specific moment. This is not to say that this was "bad training" in any way. In fact, it kept me on my toes in a way that was no doubt good for me. However, since I, as well as most beginning students of Aikido in the West, had not grown up steeped in the cultural traditions of the East, and martial arts specifically, it was not long before I found myself looking for a way to help myself "put everything in its place." I was constantly making notes, asking questions, demanding to know why all of this "stuff" was not put into some sort of orderly curriculum. Why, I asked myself again and again, hadn't someone simply sat down with pen in hand, and organized all of this multifarious information into one concise booklet? After all, Suzuki Sensei was right here, at our proverbial disposal. He understood the why, the wherefore, and the who, of all this confusion.

Why hadn't someone tapped that source and gotten all of this together for us?

After almost ten years, and countless hours of interview, discussion, travel to Japan, writing, clarifying, re-writing, organizing, agonizing, and finally layout and publishing, I found myself with a fairly clear idea as to why no one had done any of that! And that was the first manual that Suzuki Sensei and I assembled, in 1982. I hope that small effort was adequate for the time. It did seem to serve a purpose. However, we are now in our fourth edition, and still corrections and improvements are in order. Not only has much new information been added in each new version, but I think the level of approach has changed significantly. Our sincere hope is that you will find this latest training manual not only a help in providing clarification and definition, but also that there is available herein some further insight into the nature of this training that we give so much of ourselves to, and perhaps even some inspiration. In assembling this manual we have tried to provide something for all levels of training. We want to give the beginner a sense of where he or she is headed, as well as providing everyone with a kind of organized overview. In this effort, we hope we have been successful.

Christopher Curtis Maui — 2019

Morihei Ueshiba – Father of Aikido

MORIHEI UESHIBA

Father of Aikido

Morihei Ueshiba was born on December 14, 1883, to a farming family in Tanabe in the Wakayama Prefecture in Japan. His family was quite well to do, and his father was a leader in the local community. Completing his education at the Abacus Institute, young Morihei first became a tax assessor. At the age of nineteen he resigned his professional position, and moved to Tokyo, where he received his first martial training in jujutsu and kenjutsu. Becoming seriously ill with beri-beri, he returned home to Tanabe, where he married his childhood sweetheart. Shortly after, at the age of twenty, he joined the military and distinguished himself as a fierce fighter in the Russo-Japanese War.

Returning to Tanabe, he continued to engage in agriculture. Ueshiba always believed in and stressed the link between Budo and agriculture. He felt that both pursuits "nourished life and promoted clean living and high thoughts."

At the age of 29 Ueshiba led a group of some 80 individuals into the Northern Island of Hokkaido, to establish homesteads under a government program. It was here that he met and trained intensely with Sokaku Takeda, a famous master of Daito-ryu. Eight years later, returning home to visit his dying father, he met a man who was to have a profound life-long effect upon his thinking. His name was Onisaburo Deguchi, and he was the head of a new religion called Omoto-kyo. Ueshiba lived and studied with Deguchi for the next eight years. Under the auspicesof Deguchi, he opened his first *dojo* and participated in the Omoto-kyo organic farming enterprise.

It was during this time that Ueshiba became more and more interested in *kotodama,* (the power of words) which began to influence his teachings of the traditional martial art, and to inspire him to develop his own original approach, unifying the hitherto separated aspects of mind, body, and spirit. He called his new martial art *aiki-bujutsu.*

Throughout this period of his life, he continued to train, frequently secluding himself in the mountains for particularly intense ascetic disciplines. He traveled with Onisaburo to China, where they were captured by a Chinese warlord and nearly executed. It was not long after this journey that he first began to notice his profound intuitive sense. As an example, he said that he could see flashes of light indicating the path of oncom-ing bullets. One day, after a successful encounter with a particularly powerful swordsman, he found himself suddenly in a state of complete mental, physical, and spiritual harmony. He felt that he was being bathed in a golden light that poured down on him from heaven. This experience prompted him to change the name of his new system from *aiki-bujutsu* to *aiki-budo*, (from the martial art of *aiki* to the martial <u>way</u> of *aiki).*

As the reputation of Morihei Ueshiba began to grow, he moved to Tokyo and in 1931 opened his first full size *aiki-budo dojo*. More and more students came from all over Japan to train with him. However, when World War II came along he became very disillusioned and moved to Iwama in Ibaraki Prefecture to farm and study in peace. It was at this time that Ueshiba Sensei was inspired to re-name his special way, *aikido*, "The Way of Harmony with Ki." After the war, Ueshiba Sensei returned to Tokyo, and gradually rebuilt the strength of his Aikido organization. Many students began to be drawn to him. A young stu-dent by the name of Koichi Tohei quickly became his top student, was soon given the title of "Chief Instructor" of the Tokyo dojo, and eventually was selected by Ueshiba Sensei to carry Aikido to the West.

Koichi Tohei first lit the spark of Aikido on the island of Maui in 1953. Eight years later, in 1961, Ueshiba himself came to Maui, to bless the newly constructed dojo on Market Street in Wailuku. This was at the site of the new dojo that we train in today.

Morihei Ueshiba, respectfully known as O-Sensei, was a man of great vision and originality of spirit. Renowned throughout the country as Japan's top martial artist, his approach to self-development was always intense and unflagging. He was constantly refining his martial art. Just before his death, he said, "This old man must still train and train." On April 26, 1969, at the age of eighty-five, he passed away.

Koichi Tohei – Founder of Ki-Aikido

KOICHI TOHEI

Founder Of Ki-Aikido

Koichi Tohei was born in Tokyo, in 1920. As a child, Tohei was sickly and spent a great deal of his time under the care of doctors. His father, a 4th dan in judo, felt that training in the martial arts would do much for his young son's constitution. By the age of fifteen Tohei had achieved black belt. At sixteen he entered preparatory schooling for Keio University where he continued his judo practice. He trained with such ardor that shortly after beginning school there he developed pleurisy and had to leave school for one year. As he lay ill, he reflected on the human condition and his meditations made it painfully clear to him that the human body and mind were weak and vulnerable. To strengthen himself physically and mentally, he devoted much time to Zen meditation and Misogi breathing exercises. He learned Zen from Master Josei Ohta, President of the Daitokuji Temple in Kyoto, and Misogi from Master Tetsuju Ogura, one of the leading disciples of the famous Master Tesshu Yamaoka, and from his successor, Master

Tesso Hino. At the age of nineteen, he started to learn Aikido under Master Morihei Ueshiba.

During the Second World War, after graduating from Keio University at the age of twenty-three, he served for four years in the army as a first lieutenant in central China. On the battlefields where even a slight slip could mean death, he resolved to involve himself after the war in the greater game of life rather than mere martial arts as sport. He discovered that the mysterious significance of concentrating one's spirit on the one point in the lower abdomen helped in his safely surviving the war with no serious casualty among his soldiers.

After the war, he returned to study Zen and Misogi training and also continued to study Aikido with O-Sensei, now altered by his wartime experiences. O-Sensei immediately recognized young Tohei's great potential, and it wasn't long before Koichi Tohei became Tohei Sensei, Chief Instructor of O-Sensei's school. In 1953, O-Sensei sent his young Chief Instructor to Hawaii, to begin the spread of Aikido in the West.

In Hawaii, Tohei Sensei encountered many potential students, eager to learn the secrets of this mysterious martial art, but quite unprepared to grasp the teaching style that he had learned from his Teacher, Ueshiba Sensei. While Ueshiba Sensei was clearly unequalled in his execution of Aikido techniques, he never emphasized (and perhaps, in those more culturally attuned days in Japan, felt unnecessary) a comprehensive method of passing on this unique inspiration to others. However, Tohei Sensei came to believe very strongly that passing on the depth and breadth of this art required much more than repeatedly demonstrating a complex series of physical movements, no matter how adept the teacher.

He found he was lacking a way of communicating the original nature of this Aikido movement. He needed to formulate a way to approach and experience the very *principle* upon which Aikido is founded, that of Mind/ Body Unification. And so were born, for the first time, a verbally articulated set of Aikido principles, the *Four Basic Principles of Mind and Body Unified:*"

1. One Point
2. Relax Completely
3. Weight Underside
4. Extend Ki

While these four principles continue to form the basis of his teachings, Tohei Sensei, through intensive rigorous personal development and inquiry, broadened and further qualified his method of communicating to the Aikidoka of the world. From 1953 to 1993, he made over twenty-five sojourns to the West, where he spread Aikido and established Aikido training halls throughout the United States, as well as in over twenty foreign countries.

In September of 1971, he founded the *Ki No Kenkyukai,* (Ki Society International) organization, (currently known simply as "Ki Society"), in which the principles of Ki and the unification of mind and body are taught in detail. Also, on May1,1974, he established *Shin Shin Toitsu Aikido,* (Aikido with mind and body unified). Then, in the fall of 1989 Tohei Sensei proudly presided over the opening of the new World Headquarters for Ki Society, located near Utsunomiya, in the Tochigi Prefecture, on a portion of his family's ancestral lands. Koichi Tohei Sensei passed away on May 19, 2011. His ashes are enshrined in the Tohei family plot near the current Ki Society training center in Tochigi Prefecture, Japan.

KI SOCIETY HEADQUARTERS

The Ki Society was established in 1971 by Koichi Tohei. Its purpose is to teach the principles of Ki, which are the foundation of Aikido Arts, and which show the way to unify mind and body in daily life. There are many people, including the elderly, the sick and the weak, who do not care to throw or be thrown by an opponent, and yet want to learn how to relax and how to unify their minds and bodies. The Ki Society offers these people the opportunity to do this.

The power most people think they have, is only like the small, visible segment of an iceberg which floats above the surface of the water. Many have forgotten that they also have the power of mind and body unified, which is like the much larger, unseen part of the iceberg beneath the surface. Unaware of their true power and subjected to the present, constantly changing social, political and economic conditions, many people suffer from nervousness and become very susceptible to various diseases. At age forty or fifty, when a person's character is developed and matured, he should be most able to fully use his real power. Yet at this age, if he falls ill, becomes indifferent, and cannot utilize his power, not only he himself suffers a great loss, but society also loses a great deal.

One of the basic aims common to all nations of the world is to lead their young people along the right way. Still a concrete method of proper education has yet to be found. Every nation has gymnasiums to train the body. Yet no one can solve problems with only his body. Most nations have great centers of intellectual pursuit. Yet who can save the world by thinking alone? Where is there a teaching which doesn't separate these apparently divided forces, body and mind?

People practicing Aikido can benefit greatly from the teachings of the Ki Society. If we perform the arts of Aikido with only physical strength, our power is limited, and we will not be able to throw a bigger or stronger opponent. But, if we master the fundamental principle of Ki-Aikido, we will have the strength of mind and body unified and will be able to throw even big men easily. Perhaps even more meaningful, while the techniques of Aikido must not be used except in an extreme emergency, the teachings of the Ki Society can be applied in our everyday life.

The Ki Society teaches not "how to say," but "how to do." It hopes to lead many people to practice mind and body unification. It hopes to open the eyes of people to their own real, natural power and to send them to a happy, healthful life, helping them to strive for and build a more peaceful world. To train many instructors for this task is also an aim of the Ki Society.

TOHEI SENSEI ON AIKIDO

Countless people have attempted to define the absolute power of the world of nature. Some praise it as God, some call it the Buddha, others call it truth. Still others convert nature into a philosophy by which they attempt to sound its deepest truths. Such attempts to define the power of nature are no more than striving to escape its effects.

All of the forces of science have been unable to conquer nature because it is too mystic, too vast, too mighty. It too intensely pervades everything around us. Like the fish that, though in the water, is unaware of the water, we are so thoroughly engulfed in the blessings of nature that we tend to forget its very existence.

We would cease to exist if removed from the laws of nature. For instance, we would be totally unable to maintain gravity. Only those with their eyes open to the world of nature are capable of uncovering its truth. Everything springs from a sense of gratitude toward nature. Aikido, though praised as a healthful system of self-defense techniques, would be nothing apart from the laws of the great universal. The martial way begins and ends with courtesy, itself an attitude of thankfulness to and reverence for nature. To be mistaken on this basic point is to make of the martial arts no more than weapons of injury and death.

The very name *Aikido* indicates its dependence on the laws of nature, which we term *Ki*. That is to say, Aikido is a discipline to make the heart of nature our own heart, to understand love for all things, and to become one with nature. Techniques and physical strength have limits; the great way of the universal stretches to infinity."

THIRTEEN RULES FOR INSTRUCTORS

1. Aikido is the way to union with the Ki of the universe. We should set the main purpose of our practice to unify mind and body and become one with the universe.
2. Have a universal mind as your own mind that loves and protects all creation and nurtures all things to grow. When you teach, you should approach all people sincerely, without favoritism or discrimination.
3. There is no conflict in the absolute universe. Conflict only occurs in the relative world. Winning by fighting is a relative victory. Winning without fighting is an absolute victory. A relative victory will always be lost

eventually. We should train to commit ourselves to the principle of non-dissension. Be happy to throw and be happy to be thrown, and we will see remarkable progress in our practices, if we train the correct principle by supporting each other.

4. You should not speak badly about other martial arts. The mountain does not laugh at the river being low, and the river doesn't speak badly about the mountain for being immobile. Each has its own characteristics, which work or fit the best for them. Someone who speaks poorly of others, pointlessly, should know that it will come back to them inevitably.

5. The martial arts begin and end with respect. This should not be only in a visible form, but must come from your heart. Do not lose gratitude towards your teachers, especially the Founder who opened the way. Those who neglect this should know that they may be neglected by their own students as well.

6. You should avoid conceit. Conceit not only stops your progress, but also causes regress. The universe is infinite, and it's principles are deep. Why does conceit manifest in you? You should know that conceit is a cheap compromise with your self, because of your shallow mind.

7. Calm your mind at the One Point in the lower abdomen, and cultivate the capacity to accept the universe there. If you maintain this state of mind, you will

never be under the control of another. Don't cling to your opinion and fight with others. Think calmly for yourself what is right and what is wrong, and if you see that you were wrong, honestly admit it, and ask for correction from someone you respect. When someone else makes a mistake, explain what is wrong, with a calm mind, and help them to understand.

8. Even a one-inch worm has a half-inch of spirit. Everyone possesses self-respect. Don't diminish others self-respect by thinking lightly of them. The person who honors others will be honored, and the person who diminishes others will be diminished by them. If you respect other people's personalities and listen to them, they will follow the teaching with all their hearts.

9. Do not lose your temper. You must know that it is a shame for an Aikido person to lose their temper, because it means they have lost their One Point. Particularly, don't lose your temper for something personal. However, if you must get angry for the sake of the Universe, or for your country, do it with your whole being, by concentrating your Ki in the One Point. You must know that the person who loses their temper easily, may become cowardly in any serious situation.

10. Don't hold back when you teach. Understand that a student's progress is your own progress. Also,

don't hurry to see the results. No one can master something all at once. Know that teaching requires patience. You should teach others with kindness, and from their own point of view.

11. Do not be an arrogant teacher. It is a characteristic of Ki training that a student progresses by following a teacher, and a teacher progresses by leading the students. Please train together with mutual respect and caring. Arrogant people must know that they have a shallow mind.

12. Do not show your power in training, as this may awaken a fighting mind. You must teach what is right, not what is strong. Teach using your whole being. Demonstrate instead of explaining only through words. Also, be careful not to give your students bad habits by stopping their Ki movement in the middle of a technique.

13. Always perform with confidence. Study thoroughly and practice the way of the Universe, and the Universe will protect you. There is no reason to hesitate or fear. With a clear conscience and a strong spirit, you can follow the way, even if ten thousand opponents are against you.

Koichi Tohei Sensei on Maui – 1993

Shinichi Tohei Sensei

SHINICHI TOHEI

Chief Instructor
Shinshin Toitsu Aikido Kai
Ki Society

Kaicho Shinichi Tohei Sensei was born in Tokyo on 18th August 1973. At the age of 2, he started to learn Shinshin Toitsu Aikido based on the Ki Principles from his father Soshu Koichi Tohei Sensei. From 1993 he studied at Tokyo Institute of Technology and majored in Bioscience. In 1997 he became Uchideshi and started learning and training directly under his father. He also started teaching Shinshin Toitsu Aikido at the Keio University official Aikido Club. In 2000 he also became a liberal arts part time teacher at Keio University. In 2002 he completed his Uchideshi training and began teaching overseas. From this point on, Shinichi Tohei Sensei conducts a National Seminar in the United States in such places as Hawaii, Seattle, Las Vegas, Oregon, Colorado, or Washington D.C., where instructors from all over the U.S. and overseas come together to practice.

In 2007 he took over from Soshu Koichi Tohei Sensei officially, conducting seminars and workshops at Ki Society H.Q. in Tochigi and teaching all over Japan. He also started conducting seminars at companies, schools, universities and sports organizations, such as the Japan Ladies Softball team in 2008 (they then won the gold medal in the Beijing Olympics), and in 2010 the Los Angeles Dodgers major league baseball team. Since 2010 he is the President of the newly formed Japanese organization "ShinShin Toitsu Aikido Kai." He is the author of several books on the application of the Ki principles in various areas of life.

Shinichi Suzuki Sensei

SHINICHI SUZUKI

Founder — Maui Ki-Aikido

Shinichi Suzuki was born in 1917 in the small Central Maui town of Waikapu, the first in a family of ten children. He attended Lahainaluna Technical High School as a member of the class of 1934. Immediately after graduation from high school, young Suzuki began work as a laborer in the sugar fields with Wailuku Sugar. After about one year, Suzuki took a job with the Hawaiian Sugar Planters Association in soil analysis and field experimental work, where he stayed for six years.

Suzuki loved Judo play and studied for eight years with both Rev. Nishi and Rev. Kawashima of the Wailuku Hongwanji Mission. He exhibited a clear sense of leadership in the community, and when he was offered the opportunity to join the police department, he jumped at it. Through the years, by constantly applying himself, he worked himself up through the ranks from Foot Patrolman to Captain of Detectives in the Criminal Investigation

Division, and eventually to Major of Police – Central Command. He retired as a Major, after a distinguished police career, in 1972.

But the real contribution of Shinichi Suzuki to his immediate community and to the world at large emerged through his tireless dedication to the martial art of Aikido. In 1953, he met a charismatic young Aikido instructor from Japan by the name of Koichi Tohei. Tohei Sensei had been invited to Maui by the Hawaii Nishi Kai organization, to teach Aikido to the Police Department. Sensing great potential in Mr. Suzuki, Tohei Sensei chose him for an intensive month of training during September of 1953. It was during his brief period of time that the Maui Aikido Club was organized, and Tohei Sensei appointed Mr. Suzuki as the Chief Instructor of Maui County. Thus began an illustrative "second" career for Suzuki Sensei; a period of intense study, personal sacrifice, deep satisfaction, awards and honors, and teaching throughout the globe.

Suzuki Sensei was the very first Aikidoist from Hawaii to train at the World Headquarters in Japan. In 1959, at the invitation of Tohei Sensei, he spent 3 months at the Tokyo Aikido Headquarters, training with Tohei Sensei, and his teacher, the Founder of Aikido, Master Morihei Ueshiba.

After his retirement from the Maui Police Department in 1972, Suzuki Sensei returned to Japan again, this time for

15 months of training directly under Tohei Sensei. It was during this time that Tohei Sensei appointed him Head of Foreign Affairs for the Aikido-Ki Society, a position he held for 8 years.

Through the years, Suzuki Sensei never ceased in his unfailing commitment to his personal training. He followed a rigorous personal training schedule. Rising each morning long before the sun, he would sit alone at home for several hours a day, performing Ki Breathing and Ki Meditation. As he always said, if he ever had to miss a day of personal training, due to illness or travel, he was very careful to make it up, doubling his regimen on another day. This kind of dedication naturally led to an unusual level of personal development, and of course, ready recognition and respect from others, including his long-time teacher, Tohei Sensei. In 2008, Tohei Sensei awarded Suzuki Sensei the rank of Kyudan (9th degree black belt), making him the highest ranking Aikido Instructor in the world, outside of Japan.

Of course, through the years, Suzuki Sensei received many honors, some of which are the following:

— 1962 – At the 2nd State Instructors Seminar held on Maui, he received a commendation from Gov. William Quinn.
— 1963 – Received the first Maui Jay Cees Good Citizen award.
— 1970 – Received the Black Belt Magazine Aikido Instructor Hall of Fame award.
— 1993 – Recieved commendation from Gov. John Waihee and State House of Representatives.
— 1996 – Received "Living Treasure" designation by the Honpa Hongwanji Mission of Hawaii.
— 1997 – Received first Senior Tradi" award from the Japanese Cultural Center of Hawaii.
— 2004 – Received Maui Nihon Bunka Award (Lifetime Achievement Award) from Maui Japanese Cultural Society.
— 2005 – Received Japanese Cultural Center award for Hawaii state lifetime achievement award.

Suzuki Sensei was not only recognized by the people of Hawaii for his many contributions, but by the people of the world. Besides teaching regular seminars in the State of Hawaii, he traveled extensively, teaching throughout the United States, as well as Sweden, Denmark, Holland, Brazil, New Zealand and Japan.

Aikido, as it was passed on to us by Suzuki Sensei, is an inspiration in daily life. Sensei found that many aspiring Aikidoists are merely interested in fancy techniques to impress others, and tend to ignore the basics of fundamental training in which lay the groundwork for the techniques. He believed in the principle of teaching to others only that which he had actually experienced and, thus, was a strong proponent of self-discipline. In 2009, at the age of 93, Shinichi Suzuki Sensei passed from among us, though he continues to be the dynamic guiding light for Maui Ki-Aikido. We are very proud and grateful to have had such a dedicated and selfless human being as our leader.

Place slippers correctly at edge of mat

CHAPTER 1

DOJO ETIQUETTE

The Aikido dojo is the place where we cleanse and enrich our mind/body. Such a place offers effective use only when it is filled with feelings of respect, gratitude, right attitude, and positive mutual support. When you come into the dojo, you will notice that everyone works very sincerely to maintain these feelings. Any feelings to the contrary should be left outside the dojo. Following traditional forms of etiquette in the dojo is an essential aspect of our training and should be practiced with care.

You will find, if you remain with Aikido for long, that "Dojo Etiquette" is not a set list of rules and regulations to follow, but rather a living attitude. Just as discipline is a tool to use only until we learn to love the thing that is good for us, so the following list is a basis upon which to build our awareness of right thinking and right acting in relation to others.

BOWING

Bowing is an appropriate way of showing gratitude and humility, while at the same time placing one's mind in a state of non-dissension, which is necessary for right training.

When to bow:

1. Upon entering and exiting the dojo.
2. When stepping on or off the training mat.
3. Before each training session, bow to the shomen, and then to the instructor, saying *"onegai shimasu,"* which translates as "I place myself under your teaching."
4. After each training session, bow again to the shomen, and to the instructor, saying "Domo arigato gozaimashita" (Thank you), then bow to your partner(s).
5. Bow whenever requesting or receiving help from an instructor.
6. Whenever greeting the Sensei.

ON THE MAT

1. The *Sensei* is treated with respect at all times.
2. The Instructor is referred to as *"Sensei"* at all times, on and off the mat.
3. Always locate and greet the Sensei upon first entering a dojo.

4. Never interrupt the class to question unnecessarily. If you must ask a question, wait until an appropriate moment.

5. Do not call out to or interrupt the *Sensei* while he/she is teaching.

6. Do not leave the mat during class without first obtaining the permission of the *Sensei*. If you have trained during the first class of the evening, and wish to be excused from the second class, you must inform the Instructor.

7. There should never be conversation of any kind while the *Sensei* is demonstrating. When training with your partner, speak only as absolutely necessary.

8. Never argue about a technique. If there is a problem that cannot be resolved, ask the *Sensei* for help.

9. Never interrupt another student's training to ask assistance. Wait until the *Sensei* is available to help.

10. When receiving personal instruction, remain quiet until the *Sensei* has completed his or her explanation, then bow.

11. It is inappropriate for a student (including black belts) to offer instruction when he or she is not formally teaching the class, or has not been specifically requested to assist by the *Sensei*. This is an essential point of your personal development, and should be followed carefully, particularly among those who assist or teach in other classes.

12. When the *Sensei* is teaching a point, do not attempt to move ahead to another point, thinking you know what is next.

13. Make it a point to fold the *Sensei's hakama* <u>immediately</u> at the close of class. No black belt should ever have to fold his/her own *hakama* after class. You will learn the proper method of folding as you progress.

14. The formal sitting position on the mat is *seiza*. If you have an injury, check with the *Sensei,* and/or if the *Sensei* suggests, you may sit cross legged *{agura* or half-lotus), with a cushion or bench, or even with a chair, but do not sit with legs out stretched, lean against posts or walls, or lie down during class. Once in the *dojo,* you are here to train.

15. Never be idle during practice. You should be training or, if necessary, seated formally awaiting your turn.

16. All *Yudansha* at Maui *dojos* must wear *hakama* at all times while attending classes.

17. During class, while standing or sitting, never fold your arms across your chest. This denotes arrogance and a closed mind.

18. The *Sensei* usually stands at or near the front of the dojo, watching while the students practice. When acting as assistant to the *Sensei,* a student should never stand with his/her back to the *Sensei,* facing towards the students.

19. If, as an Assigned Instructor or Assistant Instructor, you wish, for some reason, to cease teaching a

certain class, you must report directly to the Head Instructor. For example, if you are an Assistant Instructor and wish to resign your position, it is not enough merely to inform the Instructor of that class.

20. For all Assigned Instructors, attending all Ki, Kyu, and Dan tests (children and adults), is an essential part of your teaching responsibility. This gives moral support to the students, and allows you an overview that you might otherwise miss.

21. Always respect the *Sensei's* weapons. Learn which these are. Never use these weapons for your own training.

PREPARING FOR TRAINING

1. Always make yourself aware of any particular needs of the Sensei prior to class beginning. A bench, chair, towel, glass of water, written notes, weapons, or anything else the Sensei may require; these must be attended to properly.

2. All Yudansha, if they are unable to attend a certain class, have a responsibility to notify the *Sensei* before the class.

3. As the *Sensei*, you should arrive at the dojo at least 30 minutes before class begins.

4. As a student, always arrive at the dojo with plenty of time to sign in, change into your gi and report to the mat at least 15 minutes before class is to begin.

5. If you are late for class, wait at the side of the mat until the *Sensei* signals that you may join the class.

6. All participants should be sitting in attentive meditation when it is time for the class to begin.

7. When handling weapons prior to the class, treat them with respect, and do not play with them.

8. If you go to train in another dojo, or another school of Aikido, do not attempt to impose your style of training upon them. Instead, try to grasp exactly what the *Sensei* is teaching.

9. When you become a Yudansha, you represent Ki Society, Hawaii Ki Federation, and Maui Ki-Aikido at all times, even in your every-day life. Consider this, and conduct yourself accordingly.

10. Never put down another form of martial art, or any other form of self-development discipline.

11. When sitting for photos, the hands should be closed with the tip of the thumb resting inside the index finger.

12. No gum chewing or eating is allowed on the mat during training.

13. Make sure your mind is positive as you enter the *dojo.* Any negative feelings you might be harboring must be left outside the dojo. There is no place for them inside.

14. No rings, watches, or jewelry of any kind should be worn during practice.

15. If you are ill or over-tired, do not attempt to train in the dojo.

16. Your body and, in particular your feet, must be very clean before you step onto the mat. Always train in a clean gi.

17. Always enter the dojo with an empty mind. If you think you know already, it will be difficult for you to learn.

18. Never come to train when you have ingested any type of drug or alcohol. The student must never ask to test, or request rank promotion.

19. Any questions pertaining to training should be referred to your Instructor.

20. All those instructing a class must attend at least one of the Wednesday, Friday, or Sunday classes with the Head Instructor.

21. Always greet the Sensei first, upon entering the Dojo. In other words, do not become involved with any other tasks or conversations before greeting the Sensei.

IN AND AROUND THE DOJO

1. Always see that toilets, showers, and dressing areas are kept clean. Do not use showers as a public bath. Shower at home whenever possible. Remember-the cleanliness of the toilets reflects the character of the students in the dojo and the Head Instructor.

2. A place of martial arts training should be kept spotless. If you see something that indicates otherwise, for example rubbish or dirt on the floor, don't wait for someone else to correct it. This is part of your training.

3. When approaching, or leaving the dojo, check to make sure that the outside area is clean and plants are trimmed and watered. Take care of your dojo.

4. The Sensei's office and bathroom are strictly off limits, unless invited in. If you need something from that area, ask an instructor to assist you, or get permission to enter.

5. If you are in the dojo, but not on the training mat, respect the teaching and stay quiet and pay attention. No books. No cell phones. Guests should also be informed of this policy.

6. Treat your training tools with respect. Your gi should always be clean and mended. Your ken, jo, and tanto should be in good condition and in their appropriate place when not in use.

7. A pair of slippers is part of your training outfit. Shoes are clumsy and inappropriate when stepping on and off the mat, and barefoot is out of the question. Slippers must always be left neatly facing away from the mat. If someone's slippers are not in order, correct it immediately. In addition, a large space must be left empty of slippers just outside the entrance

to the Sensei's office, to allow for the slippers of the Sensei and his/her assistants.

8. Ki Society Headquarters has sent a policy letter to all dojos reminding us that Aikido training and drug addiction are non-compatible. Please curtail your personal drug use accordingly. 9. There will be no smoking in the dojo.

9. Do not wear heavily scented perfume or cologne in the dojo. Avoid all facial cosmetics while training.

10. Do not leave a towel, gi, or any other personal items hanging in the dressing rooms.

11. As students, always be aware of keeping toilet paper, paper towels, soap, etc. well supplied in the dressing rooms.

12. Be aware of the dojo cleaning schedule, and plan to arrive at least 30 minutes early on cleaning nights, so that you will allow time for a full schedule of training.

13. Never compare one instructor with another. Every Sensei has something unique to share with you. Your job is to discover it. Also, do not criticize other instructors, whether they be of other schools, or your own school.

14. Any Instructor invited to teach in another dojo must first obtain permission from his/her Head Instructor. If invited, or assigned, to perform such a duty, upon returning to the home dojo, the first opportunity

must be taken to report the results of such teaching to the Head Instructor.

15. Never speak to outside people or groups regarding negative ideas or feelings you may harbor regarding your Aikido dojo or teachers. This not only will rebound upon you personally, but also will cause harm to your Instructors, and the Dojo.

16. After class it is the responsibility of the Instructor to: close all windows, check that all doors are locked, turn off all lights and fans, check to see that no toilets or faucets are running.

Bowing in and out of class

ATTITUDE

The longer I live, the more I realize the impact of attitude on life. Attitude, to me, is more important than facts. It is more important than the past, than education, than money, than circumstances, than failures, than successes, than what other people think or say or do. It is more important than appearance, giftedness, or skill. It will make or break a company...a church...a home. The remarkable thing is that we have a choice every day regarding the attitude we will embrace that day. We cannot change our past... we cannot change the fact that people will act in a certain way. We cannot change the inevitable. The only thing we can do is play on the one string we have, and that is our attitude...I am convinced that life is ten percent what happens to me and ninety percent how I react to it. And so it is with you...we are in charge of our Attitudes!

Charles Swindoll

Reading Shokushu

CHAPTER 2

KI SAYINGS

SHOKUSHU

Tohei Sensei has written this small booklet of Ki Sayings both as an aid to help the student remain aware of his teachings during training, and as an opportunity to gain a more in-depth glimpse into the ultimate nature of his understanding. The following is the recommended method of using the *Shokushu* at the beginning of each class.

1. The student who is to read the *Shokushu* in front of the class is usually selected by the assistant to the instructor of the class. If this is your responsibility, inquire of the teacher which Shokushu he or she would like read, and if no choice is expressed, then the reader should select one at random.

2. The student who is to read, beginning from the side of the class opposite where the Sensei is sitting, takes two steps out, turns, kneels and bows to

Sensei, saying "Onegae shimasu." Then the student approaches the *Shomen*, sits seiza, bows, turns to face the class and bows.

3. Open the *Shokushu* booklet to the previously selected page, or, if no selection has been made, simply open to a random place and read. Do not take time in front of the class to read through selections in order to choose a preferred one. You may say to the class, "Please repeat after me." Begin with the title of the selection, and proceed through the piece by <u>short</u> thought phrases, pausing for the class to repeat after each phrase. Articulate well, speak with a loud voice, and speak <u>slowly</u>, so that everyone can understand and repeat your words. Do not cut off the response from the group with your next phrase, but wait until they are complete. Effective responsive reading requires a clear understanding of rhythm.

4. When finished, bow to the class, then turn to the Shomen, bow, then bow to Sensei waiting on the side to open the class, saying *"Onegae shimasu,"* and exit the <u>opposite</u> direction of the approaching Instructor.

This aspect of your Aikido training is an important learning (and teaching) tool, as it helps to establish the quality and focus of the training. These Ki Sayings possess great wisdom, and should be reflected upon at length.

TEN RULES IN DAILY LIFE

1. Have a Universal mind
2. Love all creation
3. Be grateful
4. Do good in secret
5. Have merciful eyes and a gentle body
6. Be forgiving and big hearted
7. Think deep and judge well
8. Be calm and determined
9. Be positive and vigorous
10. Persevere

by Koichi Tohei

Testing Ki

CHAPTER 3

FOUR BASIC PRINCIPLES TO UNIFY MIND AND BODY

SHIN SHIN TOITSU NO YONDAI GENSOKU

1. One Point
2. Relax Completely
3. Weight Underside
4. Extend Ki

The Four Basic Principles are four ways to view the unification of mind and body. The student need only choose one of the four views upon which to bring his or her attention. All four ways are essentially the same. They are merely four ways of looking at or expressing the same thing — unification of mind and body. If we are able to gain even one of these four ways, then we possess them all. Likewise, if we lose even one of these ways, we lose them all.

In reality, the mind and body may not be artificially separated. The mind is without shape, form or physical restriction, and can be used freely and powerfully simply by shifting our attention. The body is controlled by physical laws that limit its strength and development. However, a living body is more than a mere physical object. A body that is infused with a calm mind is a body that can respond to Ki. Strong Ki can move through a mind and body which is calm and relaxed.

Testing Ki

The method of determining whether the mind and body of a student is unified or not is called a "Ki Test." These Ki Tests are many and varied, and you can find those that apply to each of the Four Basic Principles in each of the following subsections under the subtitle "Testing Ki."

What do we mean by testing Ki? First of all, in order to discover if the mind and body is unified, we use very slight pressure on various points in the body. If the student remains calm and stable in response to this pressure, we say that she is "immovable." But what does this mean, exactly? Of course, if enough pressure is brought to bear on any one place on the surface of the body, it can be made to move. If a bus or truck is bearing down on you, you certainly don't want to test your mind/body unification by seeing if you are immovable! In that case, naturally you would want to move your body out of the path of the oncoming vehicle. Similarly, if, when being tested, too much pressure is applied, the natural thing to do is to move in the direction of the pressure and allow the "tester" to pass through. This movement then, becomes an Aikido technique, or throw. So, when we are testing each other, it is essential that we fully understand what exactly is the nature of this test.

When we are going to test another's mind/body unification, we must unify ourself first. Then, we observe the examinee with our eyes, then touch gently with our hand, so feel the state of the mind through the body. If his mind is calm and mind and body unified, then we will be able to easily feel his stability when we touch him. However, if he is resisting with physical strength, or is nervous or distracted due to hoping to pass the test, this will also be apparent. At that point, we apply very slight pressure with the fingers and palm of the testing hand. The purpose here is that it also be obvious to the examinee whether he or she is stable or not.

1. **Five Principles of One Point**

    a. **A posture in which you do not focus on the lower abdomen.**
    b. **A posture in which the upper body weight falls on the One Point.**
    c. **A posture in which you don't notice your breath.**
    d. **A posture in which you can accept all things.**
    e. **A posture that initiates all action.**

There is a common misconception in the West that this "One Point" is either synonymous with the entire area located in the lower abdomen, (the Japanese word for this part of the body is *"hara"*), or more specifically that it is located just two or three inches below the navel. However, these locations are either too general, in the former case, or too high on the body, in the latter. The One Point in the lower abdomen is the point at which the entire weight of the upper body naturally falls. Locating the One Point in the lower abdomen is described as follows: When you are sitting or standing still, the One Point is the infinitely small point in the lower abdomen, located just under the surface of the body, on the top center of the pubic bone at the height of the two hip joints. It is the lowest part of the torso, where the abdomen curves under to the groin.

Keeping "One Point" does not mean continually focusing on, or thinking of, your one point. Once the one point in the lower abdomen is established, let it be. Tohei Sensei used a Japanese phrase, *"dashi panashi"*, which loosely means "leave the water running." In other words once you have turned the faucet on, (set your One Point), then let it run, (continue without interruption). If you can experience that your One Point is the center of the Universe, at that moment you will be stable. You will have *Fudoshin* (immovable mind), which makes *Fudotai* (immovable body). Your One Point being the center of the Universe, all things manifest outwardly from that One Point, infinitely in all directions. No matter where you step in any direction, you are still the center of the Universe. By understanding this, you will always be positive, and filled with calmness.

Ki Test

The best test to determine if the student is Keeping One Point is the one described in the general section on Ki Testing (that is, pressing with the hand to the upper chest while standing slightly in front of or to the left of the student), and it can be done with the student sitting *seiza* or standing. In both cases the student is verbally reminded to "Keep One Point," and when he is calm and ready, the test is applied. If he passes and is not disturbed easily, then say something like "Very Good" or "Congratulations!" to reinforce the positive memory in the sub-conscious mind. If he is not stable, then check first for the Four Principles of Good Posture (see page 62) and verbally review the Five Principles of Keeping One Point, and then ask him to try again.

As with all Ki Tests, it is a good idea to have the student try it once the wrong way. You can do this by having her consciously violate any of the Five Principles of Keeping One Point listed above. Then, try the same test both the right way and the wrong way several times, to make sure there is a clear understanding of the difference.

21

Our goal is always to encourage and support our partner. With this in mind, always complete the testing procedure with a positive comment.

2. **Five Principles of Relaxation**

   a. **A posture in which you can settle the power of the whole body naturally.**
   b. **A posture in which you relax your body without losing power.**
   c. **A posture in which you appear bigger than you are.**
   d. **A posture in which you are the strongest.**
   e. **A posture of non-dissension.**

"Relax Completely" means to <u>completely</u> release all stress from the body. Excess tension accumulates primarily in certain areas, such as the shoulders and neck. However, tension and stress can be held in any part of the body. It is one of the tenets of your training to identify the location and nature or character of this stress, and release it. A body in which stress exists is stiff and uncomfortable, is unable to respond in an emergency, and is not open to Ki moving through it.

Exertion naturally causes fatigue, as the body operates within its physical limitations. However, the mind is completely free of such restraints. It need never give in to the fatigue of the body, unless it gives up on its own. A calm mind, a positive mind, allows the body to rest and recuperate without losing any of its strength or resiliency. Therefore, a relaxed body, to be a "living thing" and not a "dead thing," must be accompanied by an alert mind. Otherwise relaxation will be powerless and impotent.

Many actors and athletes are of average height, but the best ones look "larger than life" on the stage or on the athletic field. Skilled professionals in any field are always very relaxed at what they do, even under pressure. Calmness in the face of pressure makes a person seem "larger than life." This is the opposite of someone who collapses in a chair to "unwind." A diminutive appearance has more to do with tension in the body than with the actual physical size of the body.

Ki tests show that living relaxation is stable and has great energy. A body that is tense or is filled with resistance is unsteady, brittle and restricted in its ability to move quickly and easily.

Tohei Sensei always said, "Strength has its limits, but ways of avoiding force are infinite." With a body that is relaxed and free of stress, we can maintain an attitude of non-dissension, or non-aggression, without worry. Insecure people are always jockeying for position or competing for the attention of others. When you know that relaxation, and the accompanying calmness, will protect you, it is easy to set such worries aside. Timid people shrink from conflict. A truly courageous person, with no aggression and no resistance (the two sources of most body tension), can relax in the face of any situation. With a calm mind and a relaxed body, everything is possible.

Ki Test

Relaxing Completely is a principle experienced through the body. Therefore, it may not be enough to have the student merely "think" of the One Point in the lower abdomen or of Ki Extending. In this case the student should shake both arms from the elbow down to the finger-tips (like trying to shake honey off the fingers) vigorously while bouncing slightly on the balls of the feet. When you ask her to stop the movement, be sure that she ceases very gradually, not suddenly, and that thearms are hanging loosely and showing relaxation, not tension. Then, while standing slightly to the side of the student, gently grasp the wrist on the same side and apply upward pressure directly in the line of the arm up through the shoulder. If any part of the arm or shoulder is raised, the student is not completely relaxed. Natural relaxation is a very stable feeling and should not give way at all.

To try this test the wrong way, have the student shake the arms and hands as before, but stop very quickly and with tension. With this resistant tension in the arms, the whole body of the student should react by rocking off center away from the side the upward pressure is being applied.

3. FIVE PRINCIPLES OF WEIGHT UNDERSIDE

a. **A posture which is most comfortable.**
b. **A posture in which your body feels light.**
c. **A posture in which your Ki is fully extended.**
d. **A flexible posture in which you can adapt to changing circumstances.**
e. **A posture in which you can see and feel things clearly.**

"Weight Underside" means allowing the weight of every part of the body to settle naturally at its lowest point. This is calmness. As objects existing near or upon this earth, our bodies are responding to centripetal force, or the natural attraction a smaller body exhibits toward a larger body. Of course, we call this "gravity." This phenomenon naturally allows us to move freely about the surface of the planet, without flying off into space. Conversely, the spinning action of the planet is constantly acting on our bodies with centrifugal force, throwing us away from thecenter of the earth. Additionally, we have been given a skeletal/muscular structure that allows us to maintain our upright balance. Ideally, we maintain a strong, supple body structure, allowing us to be comfortably upright and well balanced, while allowing our body to respond naturally to the eternal forces affecting it. We call this natural state of balance "Calmness" or "Weight Underside." If we attempt to push or hold our bodies downward, in order to appear strong, we actually cause our weight to move to our upper side, making us very unstable. A relaxed body, rested and full of confidence, naturally has its weight falling on the lowest side, the side closest to the earth.

Movement does not change the principle of weight underside, but it may change the place on which the weight falls. When a person spins rapidly, additional centrifugal force is created, and the weight is thrown to the outer edges of the body, away from the center-line of the movement. If a body spins fast enough, it becomes momentarily weightless, as with a figure skater. When we interfere with this small amount of centrifugal force, in an effort to maintain balance, tension is created, destroying grace and power, and creating a feeling of dizziness. Keeping weight underside is not the same as feeling heavy, but rather it is a state of buoyancy, a feeling of floating. With a calm mind and a relaxed body, all weight falls naturally underside, and we have strength and confidence in our movement.

Ki Test

An effective way of testing for Weight Underside is to have the student raise the left arm until it is straight forward from the shoulder, relaxed and very slightly bent. Then run your finger along the lowest part of the arm while telling the student to feel the weight of his arm resting there. Remind him to maintain a sense of buoyancy and lightness. As indicated above, the object here is not to have a feeling of heaviness or rigidity, but just the opposite. Place your right hand under the students arm between the elbow and the shoulder and gently apply upward pressure. The temptation on the student's part might be to push down with the arm at this time. If this occurs, remind him to remain light and relaxed and not to think of his arm as a separate part of his body. In this way, the arm is completely unliftable.

4. FIVE PRINCIPLES OF KI EXTENDING

    a. **A posture in which you do not pay attention to your body.**
    b. **A posture in which centrifugal force is working.**
    c. **A posture with merciful eyes and a kind face.**
    d. **A posture which is quiet.**
    e. **A posture in which you are positive and accept all things.**

Extending Ki is a natural condition. When you are in love and meet your lover, when you are hungry and are given a good meal, or when you are simply enjoying a quiet evening with your family and friends; these are all good examples of when Ki is naturally extended. Some people tend to think of extending Ki as <u>doing</u> something, or <u>making</u> something happen. But mind/body unification does not work like that. The feeling that you experience when you are truly enjoying something, is the feeling of Ki extending. Ki is like the electricity that exists in the atmosphere. This latent power requires some sort of generating device for it to be put to use. The mind is like this generator. The mind serves to focus and direct Ki. It is possible for the mind to intensify the force of Ki, asin directing attention, however we must be very careful how we conceive of this, because there is a paradox involved. Great power extended is a result of "insight," not necessarily "effort." Sometimes when we try very hard to make something happen, we end up getting in the way and preventing it from naturally occurring. In other words, Ki extension always happens naturally, when we feel best. And it can even be utilized in the most challenging situations, if we train ourselves to remain calm in mind, relaxed in body, and natural in spirit, no matter what happens.

Ki Test

Most Aikido students have their own favorite Basic Principle. For some, Relax Completely or Weight Underside is easier, while for others One Point or Ki Extending seem more natural. In my experience, the most popular method of establishing and maintaining mind/body unification for beginners is Ki is Extending, and the most well known method of testing Ki extension is the "Unbendable Arm."

To test for an unbendable arm, utilize the same basic positions as those described in the Weight Underside test. The student extends his left arm from the shoulder, while allowing a slight bend. The fingers of the left hand are pointing forward, but not stiff. Ask the student to imagine that his arm is a fire hose filled with the pressure of the flowing water. This is the best way for a beginning student to get the feeling of the unbendable arm. Everyone knows that, while a canvas fire hose without water is quite limp and easy to bend, once it has the power of pressurized water moving through it, it is impossible to bend. So as the student uses his imagination to create an unbendable arm, place your right hand on the top of his arm just above the elbow joint, and place your left hand under his left wrist. By holding your right hand firm with downward pressure and pushing directly up and back with the left hand, you can test the effectiveness of his imagination. If he can successfully imagine the water flowing through his arm, you will not be able to bend it. However, if the student uses only physical strength to resist having the arm bent, or if he fails to convincingly use his imagination, it will be relatively easy to bend.

Once the student has succeeded at using this basic method of creating the unbendable arm, then ask him to try again. This time ask him to imagine the Ki of the Universe flowing powerfully through his arm, extending constantly and infinitely, while relaxing the muscles in the arm as much as possible. This method is more subtle than the fire hose image, but can be much more powerful, with practice, since it is what is actually happening.

If the student has succeeded in creating an unbendable arm, be sure to try the wrong way also. Have the student make a fist and try his best to resist the bending with his physical strength only. This will be relatively easy to bend backward, and help to reinforce the right way in the subconscious mind of the student. Always finish this Ki Test by having the student execute the right way once again to retain the positive memory. As each of us practices repeating this exercise, using both the wrong way and the right way, we will become more andmore confident and adept at using the various mechanisms within us that allow Ki to extend freely.

THE FOUR PRINCIPLES OF GOOD POSTURE

1. **Your weight falls on the balls of your feet.**
2. **Keep your lower back naturally straight.**
3. **Open your chest.**
4. **Float your shoulders.**

In order to gain any one of the "Four Basic Principles" in any aspect of training of everyday life, the single most important factor is POSTURE. Many people think of "good posture" as a military type of posture; a kind of "chest out, chin in" type of posture. However, this type of posture is very stiff and unnatural, fit perhaps for the parade ground only, and a very difficult and painful position to maintain for long. A natural and relaxed posture, one that is comfortable and easy to maintain for long periods of time, is one in which, if you are standing against a wall, your heels touch the wall, your buttocks touch the wall, but your shoulders do not touch the wall. Hence, your body leans very slightly forward, and your weight falls naturally onto the balls of your feet. With this posture, you should have a light and floating feeling that promotes ease of movement, and not a heavy earthbound type of feeling. Suzuki Sensei always says, "Sit tall, stand tall, walk tall."

In addition, the Japanese word for "posture" is *shisei*, which literally means "form with energy." In English, the word "form" can refer to a physical form or a mental form, or concept, in this case a "self concept." So, to define or describe "posture" in a purely physical sense may not necessarily give us a complete understanding. The word "posture" can just as easily be referring to an *attitude*. We often refer to someone who is acting out of an obvious self-concept (such as "grandiosity") as "posturing." As weprogress more into the study of Aikido, it becomes more and more important to understand that the mind and body do not act as separate isolated entities, but join together in reflecting the overall state of being.

In order for us to possess any of the Four Basic Principles, we must be maintaining a posture/attitude that is positive. Conversely, in order to maintain good posture, we must at the same time be experiencing one of the Four Basic Principles. Following the Four Principles of Good Posture listed above, one should easily feel all of the Four Basic Principles working.

Ki Development Exercises

CHAPTER 4

KI DEVELOPMENT EXERCISES
KI NO TAISO HO

We learned in the last chapter that the condition of mind and body unified is a natural one. Later, we will see how we can practice putting this natural state to work, in the most challenging conditions, by practicing *waza,* or techniques. In order to prepare ourselves, each day, and through the months and years to come, we practice a series of warm-up exercises. These exercises are designed to develop a body that is flexible, relaxed, and in rhythm with the surrounding Universe; in other words, natural. These three exercise groups, or *taiso,* are as follows:

a. *Toitsu Taiso* (Exercises for mind and body unification). AKA "3 Minute Exercise"
b. *Aiki Taiso* or *Hitori Waza*
c. *Relax Taiso* (Oneness Rhythm Exercise).

a. *TOITSU TAISO:*

These exercises were designed to be executed with cadence movement, to the count of 1 through 8, each set repeated twice, left (or forward) on 1 through 4, and right (or backward) on 5 through 8. *Toitsu Taiso* was originally used as part of the *Shoden* level of Ki testing, but has now been deleted. However, it is an excellent exercise for practicing coordination of mind and body in movement, and can be used separate from, or in concert with, any other form of movement training.

1. *Sayu Udefuri Undo* (Swinging the arms left and right).
2. *Sayu Jotai Shincho Undo* (Stretching the upper body left and right).
3. *Zengo Jotai Shincho Undo* (Stretching the upper body backward and forward.
4. *Kenko-Kotsu Shincho Undo* (Stretching the shoulder blades left and right).
5. *Sayu Kubi-Suji Shincho Undo* (Tilting the neck left and right).
6. *Zengo Kubi-Suji Shincho* (Stretching the neckbackward and forward).
7. *Sayu Muki Undo* (Stretching the neck left and right).
8. *Ryo Ashi Kusshin Undo* (Bending and flexing the knees and ankles).
9. *Sayu Kyakubu Shincho Undo* (Stretching the knees left and right sides).

10. *Kata Ude Mawashi Undo* (Swinging the arms — alternate left and right).
11. *Ryo Ude Mawashi Undo* (Swinging the arms both together).
12. Ryo *Ude Mawashi Kusshin Undo* (Swinging the arms with hip movement).

b. AIKI TAISO OR HITORI WAZA

Hitori Waza is used as a portion of the 5th through 2nd *Kyu* testing. Just prior to the *Kyu* test, these exercises are demonstrated in motion, then the student ceases movement upon request of the examiner, at which point the examiner tests the student's coordination by gently "Ki Testing" him from various directions. This is an excellent set of exercises to use just prior to practicing techniques with a partner:

Counting Hitori Waza (Aiki Taiso)

1. Nikyo — 1-2-3-4. 1-2-3-4. 1-2-3-4. 5-6-7-8
2. Koteoroshi — same count
3. Sankyo — same count
4. Tekubifuri — no count
5. Funekogi — 1-2. 1-2. 1-2. 3-4. 1-2. 3-4. 5-6. 7-8
6. Ikkyo — same count
7. Zengo — same count
8. Happo — 1-2-3-4, 5-6-7-8 x 2

9. Kaho Tekubikosa — 1-2-3-4. 1-2-3-4. 1-2-3-4. 5-6-7-8
10. Joho Tekubikosa — same count
11. Sayu — 1-2-3-4. 1-2-3-4. 1-2-3-4. 5-6-7-8
12. Sayu-choyaku — same count
13. Udefuri — 1-2. 1-2. 1-2. 3-4, 1-2. 3-4. 5-6. 7-8
14. Udefuri-choyaku — 1 (forward), 2 (back), 3, 4, 5, 6, 7, 8
15. Zenshin-koshin — 1 (back), 2 (forward), 3 (back), 4 (forward), 5, 6, 7, 8, then switch feet
16. Ushirotori — 1-2 (pause), 3-4 (pause), 1-2 (pause), 3-4 (pause), 1-2 (pause), 3-4 (pause), 5-6 (pause), 7-8 (pause)
17. Ushirotekubitori zenshin — same count
18. Ushirotekubitori koshin — same count
19. Ushiro-ukemi — 1-2, 1-2. 1-2. 3-4, 1-2, 1-2. 1-2. 3-4
20. Ushiroukemi tachiagari — same count

c. *RELAX TAISO* (ONENESS RHYTHM EXERCISE)

Tohei Sensei has developed *Relax Taiso* as a combination of *Toitsu Taiso* and *Aiki Taiso*, (including some, but not all, of the elements of both), but with a new emphasis on rhythm and a deeper level of relaxation in movement. He has even had music composed to accompany and guide the movements. The key to the value of this music is primarily that it provides an external, repeatable rhythm to guide the student's movement. However, if the music is not available, then the set may be performed to the count of 1 through 8, as detailed below:

1. Drop hands – warm up   I eight count
2. *Sayu udefuri undo*   2 eight count
   (swinging the arms – left & right)
3. *Sayu jotai shincho undo*   2eight count
   (stretching the upper body – left & right)
4. *Zengo jotai shincho undo*   2 eight count
   (stretching upper body backward & forward)
5. *Kenko-kotsu shincho undo*2 eight count (stretching
   the shoulder blades)
6. *Zengo kubi suji shincho*   2 eight count
   (stretching the neck – backward & forward)
7. *Sayu kubi suji shincho undo*   2 eight count
   (tilting the neck – left & right)
8. *Sayu muki undo*   2 eight count
   (stretching the neck – left & right)
9. *Ryo ashi kusshin undo*   2 eight count
   (bending & flexing the knees and ankles)
10. *Sayu kyakubu shincho undo*   2 eight count
    (stretching the knees right & left)
11. *Nikkyo undo* 2 eight count
    (nikkyo wrist exercise with bounce – left circle;
    right circle)
12. *Kotegaeshi undo*   2 eight count
    (kotegaeshi wrist exercise with bounce – stepping
    forward & backward)

13. *Udemawashi undo*   2 eight count
   (swinging the arms — left; right, then both)
14. *Funekogi undo*   2 eight count
   (modified boat rowing exercise — left/right)
15. *Sayu ude-mawashi undo*   2 eight count
   (swinging arms in circular motion — left/right)
16. *Tekubi-shindo undo*   1 eight count
   (shaking wrists & hand vigorously)

DESCRIPTIONS

1. Warm-up — Start with the hands outstretched in
    front of each shoulder, arms slightly bent, palms
    down. Drop your hands to your thighs on the count
    while dropping your hips slightly at the same time.
    Do not "raise" hands but let them come up, at the
    same time as your hips, naturally. One 8 countre-
    laxed and slowly. (Always begin with the heels
    of the feet touching, and each foot turned out at
    approximately 15 degrees.

2. Swing hands first to the left, across the body and
    down as body steps lightly and the hips drop slight
    ly. Eyes and One Point focus to the right. Important:
    Do not stand in one place but move from side to
    side, drawing back the foot each time, doing the
    exercise with a relaxed feeling. Two 8 counts relaxed
    and slowly, left then right.

3. The left hand goes over the head and extends to the right with palm down, while the right hand is placed on the right thigh. Face and upper body for ward. The body first moves towards the left, weight is primarily on the left foot, left leg slightly bent while the right leg is extended to the right and straight, with the toes pointed and heel lifted off the mat. Note: Two 8 counts relaxed & slowly, extend ing the swinging arm movement through the hand over the head.

4. Use the right hand to lightly clasp the left hand. Clasp in the area of the fingers and not across the knuckles or wrists. Swing clasped hands down between legs two counts, then back up slightly behind head, looking up about 45 degrees. Do not move from side to side. Two 8 counts relaxed & slowly.

5. Keep hands clasped as in Exercise #4 with right hand clasping left. This exercise, as in #2 and #3, is done in motion from side to side. First, move to the left, throwing the left arm to the left and down-ward,right arm across your lower chest. Keep the eyes focused to the right as you move to the left. As you complete your movement to the left, draw your right foot in, keeping the heel up and making contact with the ankle of the right foot. There will be two counts to the left, then two counts to the

right, alternating until two 8 counts are completed. Going to the right, repeat what was done on the left, in reverse. What should not change, is the way you clasp the hands. For the #4 and #5 exercises, right clasps left hand. Two 8 counts relaxed and slowly.

6. Looking down and up, use the exact motion of the warm-up *Relax Taiso* #1. First two movements: look down as you drop your head downward with hands and hips, (concentrate on the chin for down movement). Second two movements: leave the chin behind and find yourself looking upwards as you drop your head back (concentrate on the hinge of your jaw). Two 8 counts relaxed & slowly.

7. Using again, the warm-up exercise #1, as you drop downward, let the head drop sideways down, first to the left for two movements, then to the right for two movements. Two 8 counts relaxed & slowly.

8. With hands lightly on hips, swing face to left two counts, then right two counts. Let your face return to center on each count. Two 8 counts relaxed & slowly. While performing #6, #7, and #8 try not to let your eyes move separately from your head. In other words, allow your eyes to move only as the head moves, not independently. Try this with a partner to be sure you are doing it correctly.

9. With hands lightly on hips, the knees bend slightly for two counts, then rise on toes for two counts.

Repeat for two counts. (Do not bounce). Repeat for two 8 counts relaxed & slowly.

10. First move hips to the left, toes up on the right foot first. There is no movement. In this exercise, count "1-2-3-4" as right foot points up to the ceiling with toes up and heel on floor. Then hop facing 45 degrees to the left with the left foot out and assume that position with toes on the left foot. Also, hands remain on hips (lightly) throughout this entire exercise. Two 8 counts relaxed & slowly.

11. *Nikkyo.* The movement of the hands is like the warm-up exercise #1. Let the hands bounce up and down. The foot movement is to walk in a circular counter-clockwise motion (walking to the left), making the circle as small as possible. Four counts with the left hand then four counts with the right hand. As you do the right hand, walk in a clockwise circle. Let the hands drop down with each count. The leg movement is quite large, lifting until the thigh is parallel with the mat at each step. Two 8 counts relaxed & slowly.

12. *Koteoroshi.* Like the *Nikkyo,* let the hands drop straight down. Four counts with the left hand then four counts with the right hand. Step forward with the right foot, then with the left foot, bringing them side by side. Then step backwards with the left foot, then bring the right foot by its side. The foot work

remains the same, despite the hand changes. Two 8 counts relaxed & slowly.

13. *Udemawashi.* Start with the left hand over your head. When you drop the left hand, let it drop naturally with weight underside, leading from the knife edge of the hand with the fingers curled in slightly, dropping hand down the middle of your body (meanwhile your other hand should be resting easily against your thigh). Use the same motion and rhythm as that of the warm-up exercise #1. Do four counts with the left hand, then four counts with the right hand, then back to the left, finishing with the right. All this time, keep the feeling of exercises #1. Now, doing it with two hands at the same time, repeat the procedure. As hands drop, allow the fingers and knuckles to touch on the way down, as both hands drop to meet in the middle of the body. Doing the reverse motion, as the hands come up the middle of the body, they again touch each other. Switch the direction of motion every four counts. Two 8 counts relaxed & slowly.

14. *Funekogi.* Looking straight forward, move 45 degrees to the left first. Extend both hands outward and down 45 degrees. Raise the heel up on the right foot. With the hands, pump them along that 45 degree line, keeping the wrists, fingers and arms relaxed. Do two counts of this, then dropping the

right heel down, swing both arms back. Do this for two counts. Repeat this process on the right side, looking 45 degrees to the right, go forward for two counts, then back for two counts. Always return to center on the last count of each side, to prepare for the change. Two 8 counts relaxed & slowly.

15. Do the *Sayu ude-mawashi* movement, like exercises #2, #3, and #5. Moving first to the left, do *Ude-mawashi* with both hands going in the same direction, making two circles to coordinate with the two counts going to the left. Upon completion, the left hand should be over the top of you with the fin gers pointed to the right. Eyes should be looking to the right. Right hand stops at the area below your belt, near your One Point. The feet shuffle to the left, finishing with the right foot drawn in, heel up and on the ankle of your right foot. Now repeat the process by making two *Ude mawashi* circles as you move to the right. Do not drag your feet on the mat. You should be looking in the opposite direction with the right hand over the top of you, fingers pointed left, eyes looking to the left and left hand stopping near the One Point. Also, the heel of the left foot should be up, left foot drawn in and weight gently on the ankle of the left foot. Two counts to the right. Two 8 counts relaxed & slowly. 16. *Tekubi-shindo undo.* Do with the same rhythm and motion for the

first four counts. In other words, each shake of the hands, wrists and arms should coordinate with a down-up movement (bounce) and the count. The last four counts, shake the hands, wrists and arms twice as rapidly as the first four. As the music ceases, slowly allow your arms to float back down to your sides. One 8 count relaxed & slowly.

Five Principles of Ki Exercise:

1. A posture in which the one point in the lower
2. abdomen is the center.
3. A posture of extending Ki.
4. A posture in which you can relax and feel free.
5. A posture in which there is no tension.
6. A posture in which you can feel the rhythm.

Practicing Ki No Kokyuho (Ki Breathing)

CHAPTER 5

KI BREATHING
KI NO KOKYU HO

FIVE PRINCIPLES OF KI BREATHING

1. Exhale gradually with ease.
2. Exhale with the smallest sound possible.
3. Exhale gradually from head to toe.
4. Inhale through the tip of the nose and fill the body from toe to head.
5. After inhaling, calm yourself at the one point in the lower abdomen.

A Zen master once asked his student, "What is the most important thing in Life?" "Truth, Master", the youth replied, without hesitation. The Master grabbed the young man's head and plunged it into a tub of water, where he held it for several moments. As the Master finally allowed the student to emerge, gasping for Breath, it became perfectly clear what is the most important thing in Life!

Of the five necessities of life, food, water, shelter, clothing, and air, the latter is the most immediately essential, and the most abundant. It is also the only one that is <u>free</u>.

47

The human lungs can take in between 3000 and 4000 cubic centimeters of air with each breath, and yet most of us only utilize a small portion of that potential, taking in about 500 cubic centimeters, as we breathe in daily life. It is generally understood that a part of our body that is not used, begins to atrophy, and eventually becomes useless. The lungs are no exception to this rule. Performing Ki Breathing, or Whole Body Breathing, is at the least, taking the time and attention to breathe completely, to utilize the full capacity of our lungs.

The human body possesses thousands of blood vessels; arteries, veins, and capillaries. It takes approximately 20 seconds for the oxygen and/or carbon dioxide laden blood to complete one entire circuit of the body. During this brief round trip from lungs to cells and back to lungs again, all the oxygen that is the essential fuel of our energetic cell engines, and all of the carbon dioxide that is the toxic by-product of these tiny machines, flows in the blood stream. How much of this needed oxygen is available, and how much of the carbon dioxide waste is eliminated, depends entirely upon how much is present in the blood stream at any one time. It stands to reason that if we have available to us the ability to fully utilize this breathing system, it will most certainly benefit us to do just that, and as completely as possible.

Breath is the key to life. This statement contains truth far beyond the obvious physical reality discussed above.

Breathing can control the autonomic nervous system, the system that is responsible for enervating cardiac muscles and glandular tissues as well as governing our so-called "involuntary actions." Next time you become emotionally disturbed, pause to observe your breathing. You will find that, like your agitated emotional state, your breathing has also become shortened and erratic. When we see someone undergoing some difficulty, don't we always say, "Slow down, take a deep *breath,* and begin again?" Conversely, if, when we sense a moment of some emotional challenge coming, we are able to calmly continue to breathe deeply and easily, our autonomic nervous system will mirror this calmness, and those related systems within our body will be spared the damage of the avoided stress, not to mention avoiding perhaps some regrettably damaging words or actions. "Control yourself, before attempting to control others", begins with controlling your own breath, and being able to control your breath only comes through hours, days, weeks, months, years of practice. So, as Suzuki Sensei often said, "Breathe, Breathe, Breathe!"

The following are the different ways we practice and use breathing in Aikido:

1. Ki Breathing or Whole Body Breathing
   Sitting in an upright position, with the spine straight, close your eyes gently, breathe in slightly,

open your mouth wide, placing your tongue behind your lower front teeth, and silently making the sound "Haaa", calmly begin to exhale. For the beginner, this exhalation may be as short as ten seconds, but little by little, as you become more relaxed and calm, you will be able to exhale for 20 to 30 seconds at a time. While this exhalation is taking place, try imagining that your body is a hollow vessel, and is, ever so slowly being emptied, as with a straw, from the top of your head, to the tips of your toes. After all of your breath has been completely exhaled gently and calmly, incline your upper body very slightly forward. Leave the mouth open and imagine that the breath is continuing to extend, to the count of 3. (Note: Never attempt to push the breath out, but simply allow the natural action of the breathing to complete itself).

Still in the slightly forward leaning position, close your mouth, and very gently begin allowing the inhalation to begin. Imagine that the new breath enters on a path up the bridge of the nose, between your eyes, down your spine, and begins to fill your now empty vessel of a body from the tips of your toes to the top of your head. This inhalation process may be shorter at first, but with experience, a slow, calm inhalation should take from 20 to 30 seconds. When you feel that your lungs are filled to capacity, allow your upper body to return to its former upright position. Continuing to hold the breath, again pause for 3 counts. Then begin this process over again, with another exhalation.

2. Retention Breathing

It is one thing to be able to remain calm, with mind and body coordinated when sitting still, but quite another when in motion. One of Tohei Sensei's favorite ways of testing this, is as follows: Sit calmly in seiza position. Inhale and exhale one complete cycle. Then inhale completely, being particularly careful not to expand or lift your upper chest and shoulders. Stand and walk forward for about 15 paces while holding the breath. Sit calmly and carefully in seiza position, and begin slowly to exhale. If you have been able to maintain calmness and mind/body unification during this movement, then your exhalation will be very even and quiet. If, as you exhale, your breath is quick and rough, then you have not succeeded. You must practice Whole Body Breathing more!

3. Cadence Breathing

Cadence Breathing is performed while walking. If you are going on a long hike, or find yourself climbing a long set of stairs or incline, practice this exercise. Simply put, Cadence Breathing is regulating your inhalation and exhalation with your steps, to a count. The amount of steps per inhalation/exhalation is not so important, (it depends somewhat upon the amount of exertion required), but as the walk progresses the count should remain constant. Ex: Breathe in as you count 1,2,3 steps; breathe out as you count l,2,3 steps. Many people, while they walk, like to chat with another person. This is fine, but not while performing this exercise. You must be quiet, and remain aware of the coordination of the breathing, the steps, and the count. This way you will find that you can walk much further, and with much less effort, than before. Of course, this same exercise has value when jogging.

4. *Haku* Breathing

Haku breathing is a very short, forceful exhalation, repeated several times. The Japanese verb *"haki-masu"* means "to throw out", or even "to throw up." So to perform *haku* breathing is to focus all of your mind and body, and throw everything into the exhalation.

First sit calmly in seiza posture, with mind and body unified. Inhale fully. Then open your mouth wide, and place your tongue behind your lower front teeth, and throw your exhalation forward and out in one forceful movement of breath. The upper body moves slightly forward from the hip hinge at the same time. It is not necessary to make a particular sound with the voice box. The breath, passing rapidly through the throat region, will create a sound by itself. But it is imperative that you stay calm and relaxed, in the midst of this great breath movement. Do not move your shoulders, your jaw or mouth area, or your head, separately. Only maintain an erect posture, with mind and body coordinated, and as the breath comes out, lean forward slightly with the entire upper body.

This *haku* breath should be quite natural. Whenever we perform any action, like throwing a baseball or cutting with the bokken, we must be breathing out. Try throwing something with force while breathing in. It is very ineffective. It is natural for our body to breathe out when exerting itself. However, if, when we have just executed a task, another task is immediately necessary, we must be ready for it with a full supply of air, so that we can breathe out as we move again. If you perform *haku* breath completely, a natural vacuum is created at the end of the exhalation, in the lungs. In this way, the lungs automatically refill with air. However, if you hold back even slightly, the vacuum will not be created, and you must suck air back into your lungs. If this happens, you will find it very difficult to repeat *haku* breath rapidly.

Haku breathing should be practiced daily. All rapid or forceful movement originates in, and is controlled by, the breath. If we learn to use this breath in a calm, but strong and lightning fast manner, then we will be able to use our entire body in this way, when an emergency requires it.

5. *Kiai*

   "*Kiai*' is an expression of the breath, and is an example of the inner nature of martial arts training; (the outer factors being weapons and techniques). The word "*kiai*' is a compound of "*ki*" (universal energy) and "*ai*" (to unite). This combination might denote a condition in which two minds are united into one. This is a phenomenon experienced by the most advanced of the Aikido practitioners.

   On an even higher level, we might say that *kiai* is a unification of the individual with the Universal. The word "Ki" is often used in the sense of personal energy, spirit, or character. This can be termed "Personal Ki." This Personal Ki is usually viewed as that which can be expressed through the average, untrained individual. It might also be what we refer to as our "life force." Whatever we call it, it is definitely that which is missing from the body when death occurs. But what is always here, what is constantly present in every molecule of the Universe, is what we call "Universal Ki." So, then *kiai*, in the highest sense, is an actual, if perhaps only momentary, unification of the Personal Ki with the Universal Ki. This kind of power as expressed through *kiai* can be used to prevent combat and win without fighting, to protect the self and others from harm.

   The uttering of *kiai* is a projection of audible breath, or voice, with Ki. It can be very loud, quite soft, or even silent. The secret to kiai is not to make a loud or force-ful noise, but to extend Ki strongly before speaking, relax the whole body, specially the throat, and unify mind and body instantly:

iei (ee-yay-ee)

There is also what's known as "silent kiai." This is per-formed by holding the breath, and extending Ki strongly from every part of the body. This kind of intense, pow-erful kiai can be used to save others from imminent danger, or to control those in an angry mood.

There is an old Japanese story of a samurai walking through the woods. He was set upon by a pack of wolves, clearly threatening his life. Instead of exhibiting fear, he calmly continued on his way, his countenance so stable, aware, and potentially explosive, that the animals were frozen in their tracks, and he was able to pass safely through their midst.

This is an example of silent kiai. As in all aspects of Aikido, it is of primary importance that the kiai be only used for good, and never used lightly.

SAI KON TAN — CHINESE PHILOSOPHY

The calmness which you find at rest is not true CALMNESS. Only the calmness which you find in action is genuine.

Similarly, the peace of mind which you find in retirement is not true peace of mind. Only the peace of mind you find in the midst of conflict is true peace of mind.

When we are in difficulty, everything around us has the potential of being our ally, only we fail to notice it. When things are going well everything around us has the potential of being our enemy, only we fail to see it.

The mouth is the gate of the mind. If you are not careful, it will spill all your secrets. Intention is the feet of the mind. If not controlled, it will carry you forthwith down the wrong path.

If let alone, waves on the water naturally calm down. The mirror reflects clearly if there is no smoke. Similarly, there is no need to make our mind clear. All we need to do is remove the things which cloud it and make it dark. Then it is naturally pure. There is no need to force pleasure if we remove the cause of suffering. We naturally experience joy.

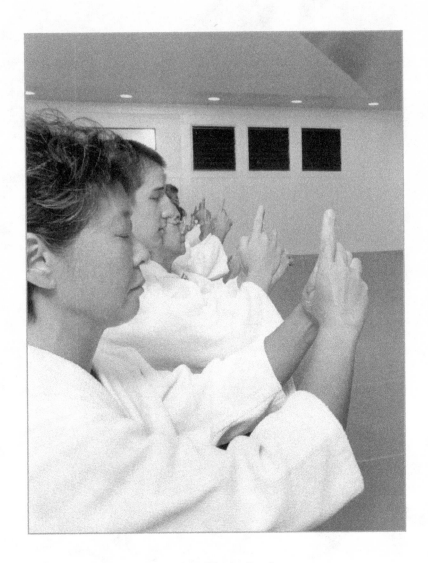

Practicing Ki Meditation

CHAPTER 6

KI MEDITATION

CHIN SHIN NO GYO

FIVE PRINCIPLES OF KI MEDITATION

1. A posture of holding.
2. A posture of letting go.
3. A posture of harmony.
4. A posture in which you can feel the creation of the universe.
5. A posture in which you can feel the movement of Ki of the universe.

Tohei Sensei calls Ki meditation *"Ki no ishi ho"* or "Ki method for strengthening the will-power." "Will Power" is the faculty or function of the mind that enables us to experience alert calmness, or attentive calmness. How this works is not always easy to discuss in words. We tend to think of "will-power" as a kind of inner force that we impose upon some aspect of our nature, in order to attain a certain desired result. However, in meditation this way of thinking can lead to very unsatisfactory results. In meditation, the more we try to "do" something, to control, or to accomplish some result, the more we will fail. It is as if we have a large tub of water that is very agitated, with many small waves on the surface. This is very much like our mind. One would never think to calm the waves in the tub by trying to use the hands to hold the water in place. We would simply wait on the side until the waves calm down on their own. When we meditate, "will-power" is what is used to keep the hands out of the waves, and allow the inner self to wait patiently on the side while the waves of the mind gently, slowly begin to calm themselves down. In other words, meditation is a process that we "allow" to happen, not something that we "make" happen.

Ki meditation should be practiced in an upright sitting position; either on the knees (seiza), cross legged with a zafu or pillow elevating your spine (lotus or agura), or in a chair. Anytime of day or night is appropriate, however the quiet of the late night or early morning is best. A place should be selected that is relatively private, and separated from where the busy activities of the daytime take place.

For some of us, this "simplest" type of Ki meditation is the most difficult of all. Sometimes this "patiently waiting" for the waves of the mind to calm is frustrating. It is the nature of the mind to want to be doing something. It is very difficult for the mind to be calmly resting. Therefore,

KI MEDITATION

Tohei Sensei has developed a very effective method of Ki Meditation. It is practiced as follows:

While sitting in the quiet place that you have selected, first imagine that you are collecting a sphere of Ki. From the infinity of the Universe, imagine a sphere of Ki becoming smaller and smaller by half, until it quickly centers into your One Point in the Lower Abdomen, and continues infinitely there. When it becomes impossible to imagine the infinitely decreasing sphere, as it disappears into your One Point, (this will happen quite quickly) then let the image go, but continue to follow, or rest in, the feeling that this process has created. This "collecting" is called *Shuchuho*. Then, after about 60 seconds, imagine an infinitely small sphere forming in the center of your One Point, and gradually becoming bigger and bigger, each time doubling in size, and continuing to expand boundlessly. When it becomes impossible to imagine the huge sphere it has become, then let that image go, and continue following, or resting in, the feeling that is present.

This is called *Kakudaiho*. Both *Shuchuho* and *Kakudaiho* produce the same feeling within, and in fact are essentially the same thing, being looked at two different ways, like two sides to the same coin. The whole process of *Shuchuho/Kakudaiho*, while keeping the mind occupied, has a very calming effect, and is an excellent practice for developing the feeling of relaxed meditation, experiencing the natural movement of the Universe.

Tohei Sensei has also developed a *mudra,* or hand position, that is very effective in allowing the Ki to focus. It is called *Toitsu no In,* and is as follows: Place the hands together in front of your face at eye level. Then interlock the fingers, with the tips of the fingers pointing towards your face, and the small, third and second fingers of your right hand overlapping the same fingers on your left hand, and just touching the finger pads together. Then close your hands, crossing your left thumb over your right, and touching your two first fingers together evenly, and pointing upward. This finger posture, or *mudra,* should be very firmly held, yet the hands should be relaxed. Once the position has been assumed as described above, gently lower the *Toitsu no In* to your lap, and let it rest there. This posture is a kind of "seal" of mind/body unification, in that, while in this position, it is extremely difficult to not be stable. It promotes a feeling of calm meditation in itself, and so is a good posture to assume when practicing any form of meditation.

Reminder: In order to accomplish anything in life, we must have:

1. **The Willingness**
2. **The Knowhow**
3. **The Capacity**

If any of these three are lacking, then we will necessarily fall short of our goal. What is that goal? It is sometimes helpful to consider that the joy and fulfillment of Life is contained within the process of accomplishing, not the result of, any great endeavor.

In addition, this "process of accomplishing" can only be truly effective when aided by the following three character attributes:

1. **Right practice (body)**
2. **Right attitude (feeling)**
3. **Right understanding (mind)**

Consider these, and make them your own.

TIME

Time is the inexplicable raw material of everything. With it, all is possible; without it, nothing. The supply of time is truly a daily miracle; an affair genuinely astonishing when one examines it.

You wake up in the morning, and (lo!) your purse is magically filled with twenty-four hours of the unmanufactured tissue of the universe of your life! It is yours. It is the most precious of possessions...No one can take it from you. It is unstealable. And no one receives either more or less than you receive. Moreover, you cannot draw on its future. Impossible to get into debt! You can only waste the passing moment, you cannot waste tomorrow; it is kept for you. You cannot waste the next hour; it is kept for you.

You have to live on this twenty-four hours of daily time. Out of it you have to spin health, pleasure, money, content, respect, and the evolution of your immortal soul. Its right use, its most effective use, is a matter of the highest urgency and of the most thrilling actuality. All depends on that. Your happiness...the elusive prize that you are all clutching for, my friends... depends on that. If one cannot arrange that an income of twenty-four hours a day shall exactly cover all proper items of expenditure, one does muddle one's whole life indefinitely.

We shall never have any more time. We have, and we have always had, all the time there is.

Arnold Bennett

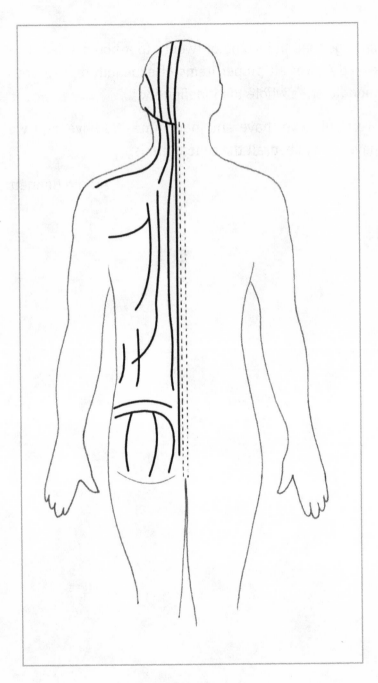

Kiatsu – Lines of Body

CHAPTER 7

PRESSING WITH KI THERAPY

KIATSU HO

FIVE PRINCIPLES OF KIATSU RYOHO

1. Extend Ki from the one point in the lower abdomen.
2. Do not stop the flow of Ki.
3. Press perpendicularly towards the center of the body.
4. Concentrate infinitely small at the finger tips.
5. Be aware of the flow, and not the points.

In the discipline of Aikido we learn how to unify the mind and body through intensive training in the dojo, as well as practicing daily Ki Meditation and Ki Breathing on our own. For most of us, this means a strong and vigorous body, and a reasonably happy and healthy mind. However, there are many people who, for reasons of sickness, frailty, or ignorance, do not have, or have not had, the opportunity to develop unification of mind and body. If they are ill or weak physically, it means that their life force, or Ki power, is at relatively low ebb. If we are feeling strong and healthy, that means that our Ki is flowing strongly. In the same way that a car with a weak battery needs to have a "jump start" from another car, in order to begin functioning again, a healthy person can help a sick or injured person by giving Kiatsu therapy, or pressing with Ki.

The human body basically functions on food, water, and air. If we have a steady supply and healthy sources of these three things we generally remain in a healthy condition. However, there is one more thing that we cannot live without, and that is Ki.

When we get up in the morning, most of us feel rested and ready to face the tests of the day. However, towards the end of the day, particularly if it has been a trying day, mentally and/or physically, we find ourselves beginning to long for the bed, where we can sleep, and rejuvenate our depleted "energies" or Ki. During the night, while we are sleeping, we voluntarily release all supposed control over our body and mind. During this time, we are miraculously filled with the Ki of the Universe. When we awaken in the morning, we feel refreshed, and ready to begin again.

But sometimes, just when we need the deep revitalization of sleep the most, it evades us. When we are ill, or perhaps worried over some particularly stressful situation or event, we are not able to sufficiently let the world of everyday life and its problems go. We may sleep fitfully, or not at all. When this happens, we rise in the morning without having partaken of the relaxed infilling that we require, and feel even more "run down" than the night before. If this happens repeatedly, then our internal "battery" has been so depleted of its resources that we become very weak. And this makes us susceptible to many diseases. We then run to doctors of the body or mind, looking for a drug or treatment that will give us back the strength that we have lost.

Many people spend their whole lives in this cycle of worry, lack of deep sleep, weakness, illness, doctors, drugs, and so on, not enjoying the gift of life, and eventually suffering an early death. However, if these unfortunate people have the opportunity to receive Ki from someone who has learned Ki therapy, they will be able to cut this "cycle" short, and revive their "battery", to allow the natural process of healing to begin.

In a healthy person, Ki flows from every part of the body. However, it flows more strongly from the eyes and voice, and most strongly from the fingertips. Generally speaking, it is beneficial just to sit with, or be with, a person with strong and healthy Ki. However, if a particular muscle, tendon, or organ of the body has become sore, injured, or diseased, we can use Kiatsu by pressing lightly with our fingertips to the affected region, thereby allowing the Ki from the stronger body to flow into the weaker. This is a very simple and direct process. However, Tohei Sensei stresses repeatedly that before and during Kiatsu, the Ki practitioner must maintain unification of mind and body, with posture erect, mind calm, and body relaxed.

Sometimes we get in the way of this simple process. Kiatsuho, in this way, is much the same as the other aspects of Aikido training. If we make the common mistake of thinking of ourselves as the"do-er", the "giver of Ki", then we cut ourselves off, and hence our patient, from the source of the Ki, the Universe Itself. Simply put, "Give credit where credit is due." If we put ourselves in the way of the flow of Ki, by taking credit, (an attitude that is often innocently fostered and encouraged by others), then our natural connection to the Universe is cut, and the boost of Ki needed by our patient is unfortunately absent. If this happens, a well-meaning Kiatsu practitioner will become quickly exhausted, and can even "receive" or "absorb" the disease or discomfort of the patient. Therefore, when offering oneself as a Kiatsu practitioner, always strive to have an "empty mind", and mentally, if not verbally, acknowledge the Source of all Ki power before, during, and after the Kiatsu session. In this way, both you and the patient will feel refreshed and strengthened, naturally allowing healing to take place.

By regularly attending Kiatsu therapy classes, you will learn the specifics of where, when, and how to "press with Ki."

Sokushin no Gyo

CHAPTER 8

SOKUSHIN NO GYO
(MISOGI)

"*Sokushin no Gyo*" (breath/mind training), also sometimes known as "*Bell Misogi*" is one of the most important of the Aikido side-disciplines. Its purpose is to unify mind and body in the midst of great effort. The essential elements are sitting *seiza*, chanting, ringing of the *suzu* (bell), Ki breathing, and meditation. When performing *Sokushin no Gyo*, the sound of the voice and the sound of the bell must be one. To do this properly, the student must give one hundred percent of him/her self to each sound, each ring. Never try to gauge yourself in *Misogi*, attempting to save some energy for later on in the exercise. Give your all at each moment, and you will discover that your reserves are far deeper than imagined. Doing *Sokushin no Gyo* regularly, the student will develop powerful kokyu, by stretching beyond assumed limits.

CADENCE:

<u>TO</u>	<u>HO</u>	<u>KA</u>	<u>Mi</u>	<u>E</u>	<u>Ml</u>	<u>TA</u>	<u>ME</u>
1	2	3	4	5	6	7	8

<u>TO</u>	<u>HO</u>	KAMI	EMI	TAME
1	2	3	4	5

<u>TO</u> hokami	<u>E</u> mitame
1	2

CHANGING OF CADENCE:

The performance of *Sokushin no Gyo* is not something executed autonomously, but rather arises from the unification of the entire group of participants. In otherwords, the striking of the bell and the sound of the voice must be one with everyone. To this end, we have an *"osa"* (the leader, seated on the right in the front) and two *"kagurá"* (the leader's assistants, sitting on the left in the front). Either the leader on the right, or the assistants on the left, should receive your attention at all times. The osa sets the cadence, or the beat, for all to follow.

This cadence changes two times, from eight to five to two beats (as shown above). At each of these two transition points the osa raises his bell high above his head, and places strong emphasis on the phrase "KAMI", as follows: (as in eight to five) TO HO KA MI E MI TA ME, TO HO <u>KAMI</u> EMI TAME, and (as in five to two) TO HO KAMI EMI TAME, TO HO <u>KAMI</u>. EMITAME TOHOKAMI. Achieving these transitions with precision requires tremendous awareness at all times. Do not slack your attention.

RINGING THE BELL

The ringing of the bell, or *"suzu"*, has undergone some change through the years. Originally, the *misogi* participant was instructed to raise the bell high above the head, with the bottom of the bell facing the ceiling, and then to bring the bell down with a forceful snap at the bottom (just above the thigh), to produce a loud and robust sound. Though this certainly produced some powerful ringing, it also required a powerful physique to keep this up for long. When Suzuki Sensei first did misogi with Tohei Sensei at his country home in Tochigi-ken, Japan, many years ago, they yelled and hit the bell for one full hour. After this Suzuki Sensei was unable to shave or eat with *hashi* (chop sticks) for several days and completely lost his voice! Not only is this forceful kind of hitting very tiring, it also can encourage tension in the hitting arm and the entire upper body.

Making these kinds of demands on the body effectively prohibited many less vigorous people from participating.

In my early days of training, it was not uncommon to see a participant break down in tears, or even pass out, due to the incredible effort required.

Currently, our desire is to make the transforming experience of *Sokushin no Gyo* available to as many people as possible. The bell should be held in the right hand, very lightly between the inner thumb and the last two fingers of the hand, with the bottom of the bell facing towards the floor. The downward strike begins at forehead level and drops to just outside of the right thigh. This movement is much like the cutting of the bokken, in that there should be as little movement as possible at the end of the stroke. In other words, no snapping or bouncing, just drop and catch. The left hand may also be used for this, but never alternate during one sitting, and choose right or left as a group. Some groups alternate back and forth from month to month. This way both sides of the body are developed. This is a consideration, though we do not do this on Maui.

Taking all of the above into consideration, one still must hit the bell with Ki power and yell loudly with the voice. *Sokushin no Gyoi* remains an extremely vigorous exercise.

MEANING

TO – SHARP

HO – SPEAR

KAMI – MIRROR

EMI – BEAUTIFUL

TAME – CRYSTAL BALL

Loose translation: "With the sharp sword of my will, I penetrate the mirror universe, and polish my character like a beautiful crystal ball."

SEQUENCE

1. *Osa* ring bell slowly, then faster and faster and finally hit 2 times.
2. Controlled breathing – 5 to 15 minutes.
3. Group chant and ring bell 5 to 10 minutes.
4. *Osa* ring bell and hit 2 times – saying "*Harae Tamae, KiyomeTamae.*"
5. Ki meditation – 5 to 10 minutes.
6. Controlled breathing – 5 minutes.
7. *Osa* reads "*Norito.*"

NORITO

Takama no hara ni, kamu tsumari masu, kamuro gi kamuro mi no mikoto mochite, sume mi oya kamu, iza-na-gi no mikoto, tsukushi no himu gano, tachibana no odo no awagi harani, misogi harai tomo toki ni, are mas-eru harai dono ookami tachi, moro moro no maga koto tsumi kekare o, harai tamae kiyome tamae to, moosu koto no yoshi o, amatsu kami kuni tsukami yao yorozu no kami-tachi, tomo ni kikoo shime seto, kashi komi kashi komi moosu.

Toho Kami Emi Tame — (5 times)
Harae Tamae Kiyome Tamae — (1 time)
Clap once

Takama no harani, kamu tsumari masu, sume raga mutsu kamuroki kamuromi no mikoto o mochite Yao yorozu no kami tachi o kamu tsudoe ni tsutoe tamae kamu hakari hakari tamaite, waka sumemi mano mikoto wa, toyo ashi harano mizu hono kuni o yasukuni to, taira geku shiro shime seto, koto yooshashi matsuri kikaku yoosashi, mat-suri shi, kunu chi no araburu kamitomo oba, kamu towa shini towa shitamae, kamuhara ni harai tamaite, ama kudashi yoshashi matsuri shi, yomo no kuni nakani, amatsu norito no, futo norito omo konore, kaku no rawa, kiyo yori wa shimete tsumi to yuu tsumi wa aragi to, shina do no kaze no ameno yae kumo o, fuki haro koto no gotoku harai kyo muru, koto o harai dono, ookami tachi ta hirakeru, yasurakeku kikoshi meseto, moosu.

CHAPTER 9

SHIN SHIN TOITSU AIKIDO

Shinshin Toitsu Aikido means the practicing of Aikido with <u>mind and body unified.</u>

The fundamental Aikido techniques are an effective way of dealing with a person who is temporarily out of harmony with his or her universe. In other words, Aikido techniques can be used to subdue a person who is causing, or threatening to cause, physical violence. These techniques are basically defensive in nature, and include almost no striking or kicking of any kind. For this reason, Aikido techniques are very popular with the police, as they must be extremely careful not to be (or even appear to be) excessively aggressive in their efforts to subdue the criminal. Even though serious injury could result from being on the receiving end of an Aikido technique, an adept practitioner is able to execute these techniques without seriously harming his opponent.

However, Aikido techniques are not practiced to ready yourself for street defense. After all, how many times have you been attacked in the street lately? The real value of repeated Aikido waza practice lies in developing the spirit of non-dissension within your self. Since early youth, we have been taught to react to apparent aggression with aggression, if not physically, then mentally, emotionally, and verbally, with anger and resentment. Often we don't feel comfortable exhibiting these negative, aggressive feelings, but we still experience them, and hide them away in our subconscious mind, where they join other such emotions previously deposited, and they age and ferment, eventually causing a general malaise or feeling of anxiety throughout our lives. But in allowing ourselves to be repeatedly physically attacked in the Aikido dojo, we learn, with the help of experienced teachers, that calmly following the five principles of Ki-Aikido allows us to solve the problem of the out-of-control aggressor, while not losing control of ourselves emotionally or phys-ically, and therefore without depositing more emotional baggage in our subconscious minds. Accordingly, ever so gradually, our subconscious mind begins to become clear of the negative, fearful and angry feelings, and our whole lives become lighter, clearer, and happier.

FIVE PRINCIPLES OF SHINSHIN TOITSU AIKIDO

1. Ki is extending
2. Know the other person's mind
3. Respect the other person's Ki
4. Put yourself in the other person's place.
5. Lead and move

Attacks and Throws

The name of an art or technique in Aikido is made up of both the type of attack by the uke (attacker), and the type of throw by the nage (thrower). The name is usually a phrase, the first part of which identifies the type of attack, and the second part of which identifies the type of throw. The following is a list of the basic attacks and throws:

Attacks:

Shomenuchi – cut to center of head

Yokomenuchi – cut to side of head

Munetsuki – blow to chest or stomach

Katatedori – one hand grab same side

Ryotedori – two hands grab two hands

Katate ryotemochi – two hands grab one hand

Katadori – shoulder grab

Ushirodori – grab chest from behind

Ushiro tekubidori – grab wrists from behind

Ushiro katadori – grab shoulders from behind

Ushiro hijidori – grab elbows from behind
Katatekosadori – one hand grab opposite side

Basic Throws:

Kokyunage – Kaiten
Shihonage – Zenpo
Koteoroshi – Kirikaeshi
Ikkyo – Sudori
Nikkyo – Tenchinage
Sankyo – Jujinage
Yonkyo – Hijitori Gokyo

PARTS OF THE BODY

ashi – leg
do – rib area
hiji – elbow
kata – shoulder
koshi – hips
kubi – neck
kuchi – mouth
me – eyes
hana – nose
men – face
mune – chest
te – hand
te/ayo – wrist

FORM/NO FORM

The three styles of practicing Aikido in the dojo are beginning, intermediate, and advanced, or *kaisho, gyosho,* and *sosho.*

In the beginning of our practice, we learn the form. We call this "kaisho." In performing this basic level, the emphasis is completely on form, with no Ki Movement.

Next, we learn the meaning of the form. We call this "gyosho." In performing this secondary level, the emphasis is still on form, but with Ki Movement added.

Finally, we leave the form behind. We call this "sosho." In performing this final level of Aikido, the form is no longer emphasized, but only Ki Movement.

Detailed Explanation:

Kaisho is the beginning or very basic style. It is done relatively slowly, and the emphasis is on the form, with no Ki Movement. In kaisho we always begin from a static position, allowing the least possible movement from the uke toward the nage, and therefore there is little or no centrifugal force acting. The idea is to lead the uke through the movement to its natural conclusion, executing with the maximum extension of mind and body.

Tohei Sensei sometimes compares this to printing with capitalized block letters. Very simple.

The second style of practice is *gyosho*, which is the inter-mediate level of execution of the technique. When per-forming gyosho style, there is again an emphasis on the form of the technique, (as in a Kyu or Dan test, or Taigi performance), but there is the addition of Ki Movement. In other words, there is now the added practice of expe-riencing the intense connection of unification with your partner in movement.

Tohei Sensei says that this style is equivalent to simply writing with more fluid letters.

The third style of practicing is *sosho*, or the advanced level. This requires the most complete commitment and awareness to perform. With sosho style, there is no lon-ger any emphasis on form, but only on Ki Movement. The throw does not depend merely upon the physical or tech-nical skill of the nage, but instead depends completely upon the degree of unification present. In order to be able to perform this level of practice, the individual must have a very high level of experience, generally consid-ered to be above the Godan or Rokudan level. Even at that level of rank, there are only a few individuals who are able to perform in this way.

Tohei Sensei refers to this style as similar to "long hand" or cursive writing.

CONNECTING WITH YOUR PARTNER

Koichi Tohei Sensei always taught us that there are three basic options that humans follow in response to a challenge, or when attempting to accomplish anything.

Option A — Struggling
Option B — Collapsing
Option C — Connecting

With Option A, we struggle to bring about a change of some kind. This struggle may involve mental, verbal, or physical manipulation, following some form of psychological technique, pressuring, begging, cajoling, paying off, or all out fighting with the opponent. When any of these attempts are made, they are naturally met with strong resistance from the partner. Generally, the strongest person wins. This is never effective, and is not Aikido.

With Option B, we collapse in the face of the challenge, and hope that someone else will handle the problem for us. Sometimes it may be a god or angel figure we ask to help us, sometimes the government, or very often a teacher, priest, councilor, mentor, or guide. In Aikido, this approach is characterized by holding very lightly and hoping for the "Ki of the Universe" to come down from wherever and accomplish the task for us. This is never effective, and is not Aikido.

With Option C, we connect intensely with the opponent, in a completely agreeable and openhearted way, and in so doing, win the heart, mind, and body of the opponent. As a result, we both move together in complete agreement to accomplish whatever needs doing. This is very effective, and is what Aikido means.

CHAPTER 10

FORMAL TESTING

A significant portion of the Ki and Aikido training process is testing, or examination. Preparing for, and ultimately performing, a test of this kind, is an opportunity to increase the intensity and focus of your training energy. It is also a time when other students and teachers in the dojo become most aware of you, and your expanding level of development. Dealing with this kind of periodic "exposure", is an important part of your training. A sword considered so special that it is hidden away from all others will never have the opportunity to be tested for sharpness.

As indicated in the following testing criteria, a student is generally considered ready to test when he or she has trained for a certain number of hours after passing the previous examination. However, it is never up to the student when he or she will be tested. It is considered one of the greatest breaches of dojo etiquette to request to be tested. It is like saying to your teacher, "Perhaps you haven't noticed, but I am good enough to take my next test."...! Whether this student is aware of it or not, the teacher does, in fact, notice their level of development, and that is precisely why he or she has not been asked to test. In simple words, if you have to ask to take a test, you are not ready to take the test.

All Ki, Kyu, and Dan ranks are awarded as a result of examination in front of fellow students and teachers, with the following exception: Yondan (4th degree) and above is only awarded by recommendation of the Chief Instructor of the Ki Federation to Shinichi Tohei Sensei, and the recommendation must meet with his approval.

Kyu and Ki tests are generally given twice per year within each respective HKF dojo, while Dan tests are administered at any HKF Seminar.

Following are the various criteria for examination:

SHIN-SHIN-TOITSU-AIKIDO
CHILDREN'S CRITERIA FOR EXAMINATION

I. 10th Kyu & 9th Kyu: Green Belt

Unification of Mind and Body

1. Unbendable arm.
2. Standing with mind and body unified.

3. Sitting seiza with mind and body unified.
4. Sitting down and standing up with mind and body unified.

Hitori Waza

1. Ushiro Ukemi waza.
2. Tekubi Furi waza.

Kumi Waza

1. Katate Kosadori Kokyunage
2. Munatsuki Koteoroshi
3. Kokyu Dosa

II. 8th Kyu & 7th kyu: Orange belt;

Unification of Mind and Body

Same as for 10th Kyu.

Hitori Waza

Same as for 10th Kyu, in addition to these items:

1. Funakogi waza
2. Ikkyo waza
3. Zengo waza

FORMAL TESTING

Kumi Waza

1. Shomenuchi Kokyunage
2. Munetsuki Koteoroshi
3. Katadori Ikkyo
4. Katatekosadori Kokyunage
5. Kokyu Dosa

III. 6th Kyu: Blue belt;

Unification of Mind and Body

1. Thrusting out one hand with mind/body unified.
2. Holding up both hands.
3. Bending backward.
4. Bending forward.

Hitori Waza

In addition to above-described items:

1. Happo waza
2. Tekubi Kosa waza

Kumi Waza

1. Shomenuchi Kokyunage.
2. Yokomenuchi Shihonage
3. Ryotetori Tenchinage
4. Munetsuki Kaitennage
5. Katatetori Shihonage
6. Kokyu Dosa

The criteria for the examination of advanced Ranks are the same as adults. There are A, B, and C level in each rank, if instructor chooses.

The applicant of 5th Kyu must have the examination of Shokyu (Over 10 years old).

The applicant of 3rd Kyu must have the examination of Chukyu (Over 13 years old).

The applicant of Shodan must have the examination of Jokyu (Over 15 years old).

Belt colors for advanced children are:

6th and 5th Kyu – Blue
4th and 3rd Kyu – Purple
2nd and 1st Kyu – Brown
Shodan

KL CLASS CRITERIA FOR EXAMINATION

I. Shokyu – over 10 years of age plus over 24 hours of training after starting.

1. Standing with mind and body unified.
2. Unbendable arm.
3. Thrusting out one hand with its weight underside.
4. Sitting *seiza* with mind and body unified.
5. Sitting down and standing up with mind and body unified.

6. Breathing exercises with mind and body unified.
First level test

II. Chukyu — over 13 years of age plus over 24 hours of training after earning Shokyu.

(In addition to items of Shokyu examination)

7. Sitting cross-legged.
   a. Being pushed from behind.
   b. Being raised by one knee.

8. Thrusting out one hand, when being pushed by the wrist.
9. Bending backward.
10. Stooping.
11. Unraisable body.
Second level test

III. Jokyu – over 15 years old plus over 48 hours of training after earning Chukyu.

(In addition to items of Chukyu examination)

1. **a.** Leaning backward on a partner,
   b. Leaning forward on a partner,

2. Thrusting out one hand and raising one leg.
3. Holding up both hands.
4. Walking forward when being held.
5. Sitting cross-legged while holding both hands of the examiner from underneath with both hands while being pushed by the shoulders.
Third level test

IV. Shoden – over 18 years old plus over 2 years after earning Jokyu.

Same as Jokyu examination, but with a calmer mind and more strict standards.

V. Chuden – over 30 years old and 5 years after earning Shoden.

Same as Shoden examination, but stricter still.

VI. Joden – over 30 years old and five years after earning Chuden.

Same as Chuden examination, but stricter still.

VII. Okuden – over 35 years old and must have permission from the President of Ki Society. The candidate must receive a special training and attend a training camp.

VIII. Kaiden – Granted by the President of Ki Society.

SHINSHIN TOITSU AIKIDO
ADULT CRITERIA FOR EXAMINATION

I. 5th kyu: Blue belt – over 30 hours of training: Shokyu exam of Ki test must be passed. To be performed kaisho style.

Hitori Waza

1. Udemawashi waza
2. Udefuri waza
3. Udefuri choyaku waza
4. Sayu waza
5. Ushiro ukemi waza (koho tento)
6. Zenpo kaiten waza

Kumi Waza

1. Katatekosadori Kokyunage
2. Katatedori Tenkan Kokyunage
3. Kokyu dosa

II. 4th Kyu: Purple belt – over 30 hours after earning
5th kyu. From here on, all techniques are performed
gyosho style.

Hitori Waza

7. Ikkyo waza
8. Zengo waza
9. Happo waza
10. Zenshin-koshin waza

Kumi Waza

4. Katadori Ikkyo (irimi-tenkan)
5. Munetsuki Koteoroshi
6. Yokomenuchi Shihonage (irimi-tenkan)
7. Shomenuchi Kokyunage
8. Kokyu dosa

III. 3rd kyu: Purple belt – over 30 hours after earning 4th
kyu: (Chukyu exam of Ki test must be passed.)

Hitori Waza

11. Funakogi waza
12. Nikkyo waza
13. Sankyo waza
14. Kotegaeshi waza

Kumi Waza

9. Katadori Nikkyo (irimi-tenkan)
10. Katadori Sankyo (irimi-tenkan)
11. Katadori Yonkyo (irimi-tenkan)
12. Yokomenuchi Kokyunage Zenponage
13. Ryotedori Kokyunage Zenponage
14. Kokyu dosa

IV. 2nd kyu: Brown belt — over 40 hours after
earning 3rd kyu:

Hitori Waza

15. Kaho Tekubikosa
16. Joho Tekubikosa
17. Ushirodori waza
18. Ushirotekubidori Zenshin waza
19. Ushirotekubidori Koshin waza

Kumi Waza

15. Ushirotekubidori Kokyunage Zenponage
16. Ushirotekubidori Kubishime Sankyonage
17. Tenchinage (irimi-tenkan)
18. Ushirodori Kokyunage
19. Katatedori Ryotemochi Kokyunage (en-undo)
20. Kokyu dosa

V. 1st kyu: Brown belt – over 40 hours after
earning 2nd kyu:

Kumi Waza

21. Zagi Handachi Shomenuchi Kokyunage
22. Zagi Handachi Munetsuki Koteoroshi (Katameru)
23. Zagi Handachi Yokomenuchi Kokyunage (Zenponage)
24. Munetsuki Kokyunage (Zenponage)
25. Munetsuki Kokyunage (Sudori)
26. Munetsuki Kokyunage (Kaitennage)
27. Katatedori Ryotemochi Koteoroshi
28. Katatedori Ryotemochi Kokyunage (Hachi no ji)
29. Yokomenuchi Koteoroshi (Zenponage)
30. Yokomenuchi Kokyunage (Hachi no ji)
31. Shomenuchi Koteoroshi
32. Shomenuchi Ikkyo (irimi-tenkan)
33. Ushirotekubidori Koteoroshi
34. Ushirotekubedori Ikkyo

VI. Shodan (1st dan) – over 60 hours after
earning 1st kyu:

(Jokyu exam of Ki test must be passed.)

Kumi Waza

1. Yokomenuchi (5 arts)
2. Ushirotekubidori (5 arts)
3. Katatedori (5 arts)

4. Tantodori (5 arts)
5. Ken(Part1)
6. Jo (Part1)
7. Four man attack (Randori)

VII. Nidan (2nd dan) — over 120 hours after earning Shodan:

Kumi Waza

(In addition to Shodan items above)

1. Munetsuki (5 arts)
2. Shomenuchi (5 arts)
3. Bokken Dori (5 arts)
4. Ken (Part 2)
5. Jo(Part2)
6. Five man attack (Randori)

VIII. Sandan (3rd dan) — over 2 years after earning Nidan:

(Shoden Ki exam must be passed) Kumi Waza

In addition to Shodan and Nidan items above, the examinee must perform one Taigi which is requested by the examiner from 30 Taigi.

The above criteria were originally developed and made available by Koichi Tohei Senseii, and have recently been carefully refined by Shinichi Tohei Sensei. Therefore, they should be followed carefully, and not altered per the personal view, or whim, of the instructor or student.

KYU RANK REQUIREMENTS

5th Kyu – Demonstrate fundamental understanding of leading Ki. Use Kaisho level.

Where is your mind?

4th Kyu – Demonstrate fundamental understanding of rhythm. Use Gyosho level.

Rhythm

3rd Kyu – Combine leading Ki and rhythm to demonstrate fundamental understanding of control of self (calmness in action). Use Gyosho level.

Calmness

2nd Kyu – Use multiple techniques to demonstrate advanced understanding of leading Ki, rhythm, and control of self. At this level, the techniques should demonstrate effectiveness. Use Gyosho level.

Embrace Leading of Ki, Rhythm and Calmness to demonstrate true fluidity.

1st Kyu – This test should show the student's readiness to train for beginning black belt level, or Shodan. At this point, the student is qualified to be assigned as an assistant instructor in classes. Use Gyosho Level.

Shodan — At this level the student should be conversant in all basic movements of Aikido, and be able to share with others an understanding of the fundamental principles behind all aspects of this training. There should be a basic knowledge of Oneness Rhythm Taiso. There should also be a personal familiarity with, and commitment to practicing the beginning levels of otomo training.

You know, as well as are able to show, how to demonstrate, with rhythm, fluidity, and effectiveness. You can demonstrate posture, line of eyesight, and ma-ai in your movements.

Nidan — The student is now formally engaged in teaching others, and demonstrating the way, both on and off the mat. Beginning levels of otomo practice continue.

You can teach others up to the level of shodan. Setsudo, clarity of movement with weapons. You demonstrate accuracy in techniques, straight up and straight down movement, and a natural rhythm.

Sandan — At this level, the student should be comfortably conversant in all techniques, and be able to demonstrate knowledge of the fundamental principles behind Koichi Tohei Sensei's teachings. Otomo practice is maturing.

You are able to clarify for other people what your teachers have taught you. Fluidity with weapons continue to deepen. There is a clear understanding of the nature of One Point, the center of the universe.

Yondan — This is the final level of tested Dan, and as such, the student needs to be demonstrating an increasingly deeper understanding of the way of being in everyday life, through movement. Otomo practice is now established as a basic character asset, and a constant awareness in daily life is apparent.

You are serving the development of others in the organization. You are teaching your students to teach.

Godan — This is a very high level, and the first level of recommended Dan. This level should be given only to those who, in addition to all of the above, have taken on some significant measure of responsibility as a teacher and leader in the Aikido community.

Must embrace beginners mind. Forget everything, including all of your accomplishments. Everything must be completely thrown away. A commitment to training and developing must deepen.

All ranks above this level are recommended and awarded under special, case by case, circumstances, specifically when greater levels of responsibility in teaching are taken on.

KI, KYU, AND DAN TESTING FORMATS:

Ki Tests:

1. Examinees to be tested line up sitting in seiza and facing the shomen. Examiner sits to the right of the shomen, assistant examiner sits to the left of the shomen.

2. Assistant examiner calls out name of examinee, examinee calls "hai", bows in place, stands and walks to front of shomen, sits seiza, bows to shomen, bows to examiner saying "onegaishimasu." Examiner says "onegaitashimasu." Examinee stands, turns, and faces away from shomen.

3. Assistant examiner calls out each test item, as examiner performs test.

4. When test is completed, examiner returns to original position, examinee sits seiza, bows to examiner saying "domo arigato gozaimasu," bows to shomen, stands, turns, and returns to original place of sitting.

5. Assistant examiner calls out name of next examinee, who says "hai" procedes in the same manner as the first examinee.

6. Once all Ki Tests are completed, assistant examiner and examiner review test sheets, and then examiner stands and informs the group of examinees who has passed or has not passed.

Kyu Tests: (hitori waza will be completed prior to kyu test)

1. Examinees to be tested line up sitting in seiza and facing the shomen. Examiner sits to the right of the shomen, assistant examiner sits to the left of the shomen.
2. Assistant examiner calls out name of examinee and test to be taken, examinee calls "hai," both examinee and test partner bow in place, stand and move to testing position (approx. 12 ft. or 4 meters apart), sit seiza facing shomen. Assistant examiner calls "shomen ni, rei" and the two partners bow to shomen, then "sensei ni, rei" and they bow to examiner, then "otagai ni, rei" and they bow to each other.
3. At conclusion of Kyu test, partners sit seiza facing each other, assistant examiner calls "otagai ni, rei" and they bow to each other, "sensei ni, rei" and they bow to the examiner, and "shomen ni, rei" and they bow to the shomen.
4. As the examinee and partner make this last bow, the assistant examiner calls the name and test of the next examinee, so that the previous examinee

and partner and next examinee and partner stand at the same time, so that both are moving at the same time, one towards the shomen, one away from the shomen.

Dan Tests:

1. Examinees to be tested line up sitting seiza and facing the shomen. Examiner sits to the right of the shomen, examiner sits to the left of the shomen.
2. Assistant examiner calls out name of examinee and test to be taken, examinee calls "hai," both examinee and test partner bow in place, stand and move to testing position (approx. 12' or 4 meters apart), sit seiza facing the shomen. On their own the two partners bow to shomen, then face each other, bow to each other, and begin the test arts. They will perform these test arts on one side only. This can be done all on left side, all on right side, or alternating.
3. If the examinee is taking the Sandan test, then the final section of arts before weapons will be the selected Taigi. While performing the Taigi, the examinee and uke will perform all arts on both right and left sides.
4. When the test arts are completed, both sit seiza facing each other, they bow to each other, and the partner exits to retrieve the bokken for the examinee.

5. The examinee sits seiza with bokken facing the shomen, bows, and begins. He performs bokken kata once, at regular speed and full voice, counting in Japanese.

6. When kata is completed, examinee finishes in a sitting position, and exchanges bokken for jo with partner while sitting and facing shomen.

7. Then the examinee bows and begins. He performs the jo kata once, at regular speed with full voice, counting in Japanese.

8. When this is completed, the examinee sits seiza, bows to shomen, gives jo to partner who returns it to side of mat.

9. If examinee is performing both Ken 1 & 2 and Jo 1 & 2, then move smoothly from one to the next without pause. In example, "ni ju ichi, ni ju ni, ichi." So continuing right on from Jo 1 to Jo 2.

10. Examinee sits facing the shomen to begin randori. The randori uke enter in a line and sit facing shomen (24' or 8 meters from examinee).

11. The examiner calls "shomen ni, rei," then all participants bow to shomen, "otagai ni, rei," then all uke bow to examinee.

12. Before head of examinee rises from bow, the examiner calls "hajime" and the randori begins. (There is no longer a requirement for any sudori during the randori).

13. When the examiner feels the randori has been completed, he calls "yame" and the examinee and the uke all return to sit in original positions.

14. Examiner calls "otagai ni, rei," then all participants bow to each other, "shomen ni, rei" and all participants bow to shomen, rise and exit the mat in orderly manner.

CHAPTER 11

TAIGI ARTS

The Taigi arts were developed by Koichi Tohei Sensei to help promote precision and grace in the movement of both the *nage* and the *uke,* as well as to encourage both participants to remain calm and mutually unified for an extended period of time. You will notice that these organized series of techniques are to be performed within a specific framework of time, not less nor more than the number of seconds allowed. This provides the student with a kind of guideline to which he or she may compare his or her execution. If the Taigi techniques are performed with the appropriate rhythm and timing, then the length of execution will match that suggested. It may be interesting to note that most commonly the arts are performed too <u>rapidly,</u> not too <u>slowly.</u>

For more than 20 years, Ki Society World Headquarters in Japan held annual "Taigi Competitions" for adults and college age students. The "competitions" are not designed to promote direct competition between the students, but to encourage the student to compete against his own, past best effort. While participating in a series of these competitions, the student, with the help of the qualified judges, is able to easily see his progress from one level to another. All performers are required to perform the mandatory ' *Kitei Taigi* '. In addition, the participants must choose a minimum of one taigi from a list of *"sentaku"*, or selections, that is provided by Ki Society HQ, and changes each year. The judging is done on a point system, much like pairs ice-skating is judged. There is never any opportunity to win by "beating" any other participant, but only by demonstrating to the judges a high level of competence in the execution of the waza or technique.

It should be noted that the opportunity to earn or lose the most points is not in the specific execution of each technique, but rather in the overall qualities of stability, rhythm, and fullness or largeness of Ki.

The following is a list of the 30 Taigi, together with the allotted time allowed for each one. The participants should strive to complete each series, with both a right and a left hand attack, within 2 seconds more or less of the stated time.

Currently, the Taigi Competition is held exclusively for young adults.

KITEI TAIGI 110 SECONDS

1. Shomenuchi Kokyunage
2. Yokomenuchi Shihonage
3. Munetsuki Koteoroshi
4. Katatedori Ikkyo Tenkan
5. Katadori Nikkyo Irimi
6. Ushiro-tekubidori Sankyo (Katameru)

1. Daiichi Taigi Katatedori (Shodan)   65 sec

1. Katatedori Kokyunage Tenkan
2. Katatedori Kirikaeshi Tenkan
3. Katatedori Zenpo Nage Tenkan
4. Katatedori Kaiten Nage Tenkan
5. Katatedori Shihonage Tenkan
6. Katatedori Ikkyo Tenkan

2. Daini Taigi Katatedori Ryotemochi (Nidan)   71 sec

1. Katatedori Ryotemochi Kokyunage Tenkan (Jump in)
2. Katatedori Ryotemochi Kokyunage Tenkan (circle)
   Katatedori Ryotemochi Kokyunage Tenkan (figure 8)
3. Katatedori Ryotemochi Zenpo Nage Tenkan
   (up and down)
4. Katatedori Ryotemochi NikkyTenkan (hold uke's
   fingers first – rotate uke)
5. Katatedori Ryotemochi Koteoroshi Tenkan (one
   scoop and lock)

3. Daisan Taiqi Yokomenuchi (Sandan)   49 sec

1. Yokomenuchi Sudori (go in turn back and slide out)
2. Yokomenuchi Sudori (ojiki – bow)
3. Yokomenuchi Kokyunage lrimi (cut neck and throw)
4. Yokomenuchi Shihonage lrimi (regular)
5. Yokomenuchi Kokyunage Sudori Nage (one hand over head throw forward).
6. Yokomenuchi Kokyunage Tenkan (figure 8)

*NOTE: Do Numbers 1 to 3 with right hand one after the other and then do the left side in the same manner.

4. Daiyon Taigi Ryokatadori – Women's Art   60 sec

1. Ryokatadori Kokyunage Tenkan (turn and bow)
2. Ryokatadori Kokyunage Tenkan (kirikaeshi)
3. Ryokatadori Kokyunage Tenkan (bow and bow)
4. Ryokatadori Sudori
5. Ryokatadori Nikkyo Tenkan
6. Ryokatadori Zenpo Nage (cut neck and throw)

5. Daigo Taigi – Children's Art   77 sec

1. Shomenuchi Kokyunage
2. Yokomenuchi Shihonage
3. Munetsuki Koteoroshi
4. Katadori lkkyo (irimi)
5. Kokyu Dosa.

6. Dairoku Taigi Ushiro Waza – Retirees Over 60 71 sec

1. Ushirodori Kokyunage (throw forward)
2. Ushirotekubidori Kokyunage Tenkan (Uragaeshi)
3. Ushirotekubidori Zenpo Nage
   (grab one hand, dip down and over head and over
   one shoulder and throw forward)
4. Ushirotekubidori oteoroshi (Hantai tenkan)
5. Ushirotekubidori Ikkyu (tenkan)
6. Ushirotekubidori Sankyo (irimi)

7. Dainana Taigi Munetsuki and Kick – University Students   66 sec

1. Munetsuki Kokyunage (cut neck)
2. Munetsuki Ikkyo Hantai Tenkan (opposite hand)
3. Munetsuki Zenpo Nage
4. (outside – hold under uke's arm and throw forward)
5. Maegeri Kokyunage Irimi (block kick and hit face)
6. Mawashigeri Kokyunage (side kick, catch leg back-
   side and throw uke backward)
7. Munetsuki Koteoroshi (throw uke far and high)

8. Daihachi Taigi Ryotedori   50 sec

1. Ryotedori Tenchinage Irimi
2. Ryotedori Tenchinage Tenkan
3. Ryotedori Kokyunage (swan lake – yurei nage)
   Ryotedori Kokyunage (sayu undo)

4. Ryotedori Kokyunage Zenpo Nage (forward)
5. Ryotedori Kokyunage Kirikaeshi

9. <u>Daikyu Taigi Shomenuchi</u>   67 sec

1. Shomenuchi lkkyo lrimi (do not grab hand)
2. Shomenuchi lkkyo Tenkan
3. Shomenuchi Kokyunage (banzai throw)
4. Shomenuchi Koteoroshi
5. Shomenuchi Kokyunage Kirikaeshi
6. Shomenuchi Kokyunage Zenpo Nage (throw forward under arm)

10. <u>Daiju Taiai Katadori Shomenuchi</u>   65 sec

1. Katadori Menuchi Kokyunage lrimi (no touch art)
2. Katadori Menuchi Kokyunage Tenkan (circle)
3. Katadori Menuchi Kokyunage Tenkan (figure 8)
4. Katadori Menuchi lkkyo Tenkan
5. Katadori Menuchi Kokyunage (sankyo style)
6. Katadori Menuchi Kokyunage Zenpo Nage (throw forward)

11. <u>Daijuichi Taigi Katatedori</u>   56 sec

1. Katatedori Kokyunage lrimi (no touch art)
2. Katatedori Kokyunage Irimi/Tenkan
3. Katatekosadori Kokyunage Tenkan

4. Katatekosadori Kokyunage (curl wrist)
5. Katatekosadori Kokyunage lrimi (curl wrist – no touch art)
6. Katatekosadori Kokyunage Kirikaeshi

12. Daijuni Taiqi Katatedori Ryotemuchi   66 sec

1. Katatedori Ryotemochi Kokyunage lrimi (no touch art – elbow down and up)
2. Katatedori Ryotemochi Kokyunage Tenkan
3. Katatedori Ryotemochi Kokyunage Nikkyo (mawashi style)
4. Katatedori Ryotemochi Kokyunage Ikkyo/Kirikaeshi
5. Katatedori Ryotemochi Kokyunage Zenpo Nage
6. Katatedori Ryotemochi Kokyunage (Ball Nage)

13. Daijusan Taiqi Yokomenuchi   61 sec

1. Yokomenuchi Kokyunage lrimi
2. Yokomenuchi Kokyunage Juji lrimi Nage
3. Yokomenuchi Kokyunage Atemi
4. Yokomenuchi Shihonage lrimi Tobikomi
5. Yokomenuchi Koteoroshi (undo)
6. Yokomenuchi Kokyunage Zenpo Nage, Kirikaeshi

14. Daijuyon Taiqi Katadori   1 min 25 sec

1. Katadori lkkyo Tenkan
2. Katadori Nikkyo lrimi
3. Katadori Sankyo Tenkan
4. Katadori Yonkyo lrimi
5. Katadori Kokyunage Ushiromuki, Bow
6. Katadori Kokyunage Kirikaeshi, Ushiromuki
   (Yokomenuchi)

15. Daijugo Taigi – Intermediate School   1 min 29 sec

1. Shomenuchi lkkyo lrimi
2. Yokomenuchi Kokyunage Tenkan (figure 8)
3. Munetsuki Zenpo Nage
4. Katadori Nikkyo lrimi
5. Ushirodori Kokyunage Zenpo Nage
6. Ushirotekubidori Sankyo Nage

16. Daijuroku Taigi Zagi   60 sec

1. Shomenuchi lkkyo lrimi
2. Shomenuchi lkkyo Tenkan
3. Shomenuchi Kokyunage
4. Katadori Shomenuchi Kokyunage lrimi
5. Munetsuki Koteoroshi
6. Yokomenuchi Kokyunage

17. Daijunana Taigi Zagi Handachi   54 sec

1. Katatedori Kokyunage
2. Katatedori Kokyunage Kirikaeshi
3. Shomenuchi Kokyunage
4. Ushirokatadori Kokyunage
5. Munetsuki Koteoroshi
6. Yokomenuchi Kokyunage

18. Daijuhachi Taigi Ushiro Waza   72 sec

1. Ushirodori Kokyunage Hagaijim (hold elbows from back)
2. Ushiro Katadori Kokyunage Hikoki (air-plane) Nage
3. Ushiro Katadori Kokyunage Hikoki Kirikaeshi
4. Ushiro Katadori Kokyunage Zenpo Nage
5. Ushiro Katatedori Kubishime Uragaeshi (inside out) Kokyunage
6. Ushiro Katatedori Kubishime Zenpo Nage

19. Daijuku Taigi Munetsuki   52 sec

1. Munetsuki Kokyunage Uchiwanage Kubikiri (fan)
2. Munetsuki Kokyunage Zenpo Nage Yokomenuchi
3. Munetsuki Kokyunage Uchiwanage Menuchi
4. Munetsuki Kokyunage Irimi Sudori
5. Munetsuki Kokyunage Shomenuchi
6. Munetsuki Kokyunage Hantai Tenkan

20. Dainiju Taigi Futari Sannin Waza   82 sec

1. Futari Ryotemochi Kokyunage Zenpo Nage (1 time)
2. Futari Ryotemochi Kokyunage Senaka Awase (1 time)
3. Futari Ryotemochi Kokyunage Seiretsu (1 time)
4. Futari Ryotemochi Shihonage
5. Sannin Ryotemochi Kokyunage Seiretsu
6. Sanningake Randori

21. Dainijuichi Taigi Tanken Dori   2min 11sec

1. Shomenuchi Koteoroshi
2. Shomenuchi Kokyunage
3. Yokomenuchi Irimi Sakate
4. Yokomenuchi Kokyunage Gokyo (sakate)
5. Yokomenuchi Shihonage
6. Munetsuki Koteoroshi
7. Munetsuki Ikkyo Irimi
8. Munetsuki Kokyunage Zenpo Nage
9. Munetsuki Hiji Menuchi
10. Munetsuki Kaiten Nage

22. Dainijuni Taigi Tachi Dori (Bokken Dori) 1 min 46 sec

1. Shomenuchi Irimi Sudori
2. Shomenuchi Koteoroshi (right only)
3. Shomenuchi Irimi Dori (left only)
4. Yokomenuchi Kokyunage Irimi

5. Yokomenuchi Shihonage (left only)
6. Munetsuki Koteoroshi (right only)
7. Munetsuki Kokyunage Zenpo Nage
8. Douchi Kokyunage
9. Yokobarai Kokyunage

23. Dainijusan Taigi Jo Dori   2 min 4 sec

1. Shomenuchi lrimi Sudori
2. Shomenuchi Koteoroshi (right only)
3. Shomenuchi lrimidori (left only)
4. Yokomenuchi Shihonage (left only)
5. Yokomenuchi Kokyunage Zenpo Nage
6. Munetsuki Kokyunage Tsukikaeshi
7. Munetsuki Kokyunage Zenpo Nage
8. Munetsuki Kokyunage Kirikaeshi
9. Douchi Kokyunage
10. Yokobarai kokyunage

24. Dainijuyon Taigi Jo Nage   68 sec

1. Kokyunage
2. Kakyunage Zenpo Nage
3. Sakate Mochi Kokyunage Zenpo Nage
4. Shihonage
5. Nikkyo
6. Koteoroshi
7. Kokynage Kirikaeshi
8. Kokyunage Ashi Sukui (Ashi Barai)

25. <u>Dainijugo Taigi Ken (Sword) #1</u>   **27 sec**

1. Happo Giri

26. <u>Dainijuroku Taigi Ken (Sword) #2</u>   **29 sec**

1. Ichinotachi
2. Hidari Kesagiri
3. Migi Kesagiri
4. Ushiro Uchi
5. Tsuki
6. Ushiro Uchi
7. Tsuki
8. Hidari Kesagake Tobi komi
9. Migi Kesagake Tobi Komi
10. Tsuki
11. Hidari Kesagake

27. <u>Dainijunana Taigi Jo #1</u>   **38 sec**

1. 22 Counts

28. <u>Dainijuhachi Taigi Jo # 2</u>   **40 sec**

1. Tsuki Zujo (continued)
2. Tsuki Zujo
3. Hidari Yokomenuchi
4. Mawashite Migi Uchi Oroshi

5. Migi Yokomenuchi
6. Tsuki Zujo – Ushiro Muki
7. Hidari Yokomenuchi
8. Mawashite Migi Oroshi
9. Migi Yokomenuchi
10. Tsukį Zujo – Ushiromuki
11. Hidari Yokomenuchi
12. Hidari Kohotsuki (ushiro)
13. Migi Kohotsuki Ushiro Muki
14. Tsuki – Ushiromuki
15. Fumikonde (Hidari) Yokomenuchi
16. Isen Kai Kiri Harai Zujyo (circle)
17. Migishitakara
18. Tsuki
19. Migi Yokomenuchi
20. Tsuki
21. Hidari Ashi Sagari Migishitakara Hidari Harai Age
22. Mochi Kaete Tsuki

29. Dainijuku Taigi Tachi Uchi Ken

1. Koteuchi
2. Migi Douchi
3. Hidari Douchi
4. Nodo Tsuki
5. Shomenuchi
6. Hidari Yokomenuchi – Migi Yokomenuchi

30. <u>Daisanju Taigi Shinken Kokoro No Ken</u>

1. Shomenuchi
2. Hidari Ashi Maeuchi – Ushiro Uchi
3. Migi Ashi Maeuchi – Ushiro Uchi
4. Hidari Yokomenuchi – Rensoku (continue)
5. Migi Yokomenuchi
6. Hidari Kesa Ashi Barai
7. Migi Kesa Ashi Barai

CHAPTER 12

BOKKEN AND JO

WOODEN SWORD AND WOODEN STAFF

FIVE PRINCIPLES OF KEN WITH KI

1. Hold the bokken lightly.
2. The tip of a bokken must be calm.
3. Use the weight of a bokken.
4. Do not lose your attention.
5. Mind moves first.

FIVE PRINCIPLES OF JO WITH KI

1. Hold the jo lightly.
2. Hold with the hand closest to your body.
3. Move the jo freely.
4. Always keep one hand on a jo when moving.

The Taigi techniques for *Bokken* and *Jo* listed in the previous chapter involve the art of disarming an attacker, as well as demonstrations of handling of the weapons themselves.

However, before we can ever learn to move with a four to six foot sword or staff in our hands, we must first learn to become one with that instrument; to make that weapon feel and look as if it is a part of our mind and body, not a separate entity or foreign object. Therefore, how we treat the ken or jo is of the utmost importance. The Japanese look at the sword not as a weapon of destruction, but as an object of inspiration. The sword must be respected at all times, for it acts as a mirror of our mind. When picking up the *bokken,* when sitting with it, walking with it, handing it to someone, or when using it in any way, it must be treated as though it is part of your mind and body.

All weapons training begins and ends with standing in ready position *(Hanmi* position or *sankaku no kamae* — triangular stance) while holding the weapon calmly and steadily. When standing in this position, with mind and body unified and the tip of the weapon being the central point of the triangle, it is virtually impossible for an opponent to reach your body with his or her weapon. The opponent would be forced to move the long way around your triangle and come to you from the side, while you would be able to move directly, in a straight line, into your opponent. This position is therefore a perfect defense in itself, requiring no movement if held properly.

You will learn the various positions and movement sequences and variations from the instructors as you progress in your training through the months and years.

However the importance of practicing with a *bokken* or *jo* is not to learn how to wield a weapon. After all, in this day and age, what possibility is there that you would ever need to use such a weapon in daily life? But you do use all manner of objects and tools in whatever work or chores you perform each day. Practicing sincerely with *bokken* and *jo,* we can learn the principle of putting all of our mind and body into whatever we are holding or using, whether it be a pen, a kitchen knife, or a golf club.

PARTS OF SWORD

tsuka – handle
tsuba – hilt
saya – scabbard
toshin – blade
ha – cutting edge
shinogi – back of blade

KAMAE—POSITIONS

chudan kamae – chest high
gedan kamae – hands at waist, tip 12"to 18" from floor
waki gamae – same as *gedan,* except to the side
  right = *migi,* left = *hidari*
hasso gamae – to the side of head, tip up right = *migi,*
  left = *hidari*
jodan kamae – above head

NAMES OF VARIOUS LENGTH WEAPONS

tanto, tanken — knife
wakizashi, shoto — short sword
katana — sword
tachi — long sword
bokken — wooden sword
jo, bo — wooden staff

SUBURI

#1 — Kamae (count 1 — 12)

1. Chudan Kamae — step back with left foot.
2. Gedan Kamae — left, then right foot slides back slightly.
3. Right Waki Gamae — step back with right foot.
4. Right Hasso Gamae — right foot move forward slightly.
5. Right Jodan Kamae — step forward with right foot.
6. Chudan Kamae — maintain same foot positions.
7. Left Jodan Kamae — step forward with left foot.
8. Gedan Kamae — step back with left foot.
9. Left Waki Gamae — slide left foot back slightly.
10. Left Hasso Gamae — slide left foot forward slightly.
11. Left Jodan Kamae — step forward with left foot.
12. Chudan Kamae — step back with left foot.

#2 – Repetitive cutting:

1. Shomen kiri – right and left)
2. Kesagiri – (right and left)
3. Waki gamae – (right and left)
4. Hasso gamae – (right and left)
5. Tsuki – (right, left, and straight)
6. Kiriage – (right and left)
7. Yokogiri – (right and left)
8. Kirikaeshi – (right and left)
9. Tsubame kiri – right and left)
10. Shin choku giri – (high and low)

#3 – One hand cutting: Right, left with ten count

#4 – Kesagiri: Right, left, center with kiai

#5 – Tsuki: Right, left, with ten count

#6 – Kesagiri plus tsuki: Right, left, center, tsuki; then left, right, center, tsuki with eight count

#7 – Gedan kamae, right waki gamae, chudan kamae, left waki gamae, chudan kamae, right hasso gamae, right kesagiri, left hasso gamae, left kesagiri, right tsuki (means blade faces to the right), cut shomen to chudan kamae with left foot forward, step forward on right foot and make straight tsuki, with twelve count.

#8 — Kiriage: (14 counts)

1. Drop tip to gedan kamae while sliding left foot back slightly.
2. Move bokken back to migi waki gamae, while stepping back with right foot.
3. Cut upwards in kiriage move, without moving feet.
4. Move right foot forward & cut to chudan kamae.
5. Move blade back to hidari waki gamae.
6. Cut upwards in kiriage move, without moving feet.
7. Cut to chudan kamae without moving feet.
8. Move bokken back to migi waki gamae, while stepping back with right foot.
9. Cut upwards in kiriage move, without moving feet
10. Move right foot forward & cut to chudan kamae.
11. Move blade back to hidari waki gamae.
12. Cut upwards in kiriage move, without moving feet.
13. Move slightly forward and to the left and cut shin choku giri.
14. Step back slightly and to the right and return to chudan kamae.

#9 — Yokogiri: (12 counts)

1. Drop tip to gedan kamae while sliding left foot back slightly.
2. Move blade back to migi waki gamae.
3. Raise bokken to hip level and cut yokogiri from right to left across body without moving feet.

4. Step forward with right foot and cut to chudan kamae.
5. Move bokken back to hidari waki gamae, while stepping back with left foot.
6. Raise bokken to hip level and cut yokogiri from left to right across body without moving feet.
7. Cut kirikaeshi front and back.
8. Cut kirikaeshi back and front.
9. Cut migi tsubame kiri.
10. Cut hidari tsubame kiri.
11. Move slightly forward and to the left and cut shin choku giri.
12. Step back slightly and to the right and return to chudan kamae.

#10 – Yokogiri, kesagiri (14 counts)

1. Cut shomen
2. Thrust tsuki (leaving blade down for tsuki)
3. Cut yokogiri from left to right across body.
4. Move bokken down to migi waki gamae, while stepping back with right foot.
5. Cut upwards in kiriage move, without moving feet.
6. move blade to jodan kamae.
7. Cut left kesagiri.
8. Cut yokogiri from right to left across body.
9. Drop bokken to left hidari waki gamae position.
10. Cut upwards in kiriage move, without moving feet.

11. Move blade to jodan kamae.
12. Cut right kesagiri.
13. Move slightly forward and to the left and cut shin choku giri.
14. Step forward slightly and to the right and return to chudan kamae.

KATA

There are two sets of exercise sequences, or *kata,* practiced with the *bokken,* known as *Bokken* #1 and *Bokken* #2 and two sets for the *Jo,* called *Jo* #1 and *Jo* #2. All counting for these *kata* are done in Japanese, as the movements are designed to flow with the sounds and rhythm of that language. The idea is that the sound of the voice and the movement of the body are executed as one. This means that the impulse for both voice and movement arise from the One Point simultaneously. This necessarily involves breath control. Following are the four sequences showing the count. The exact physical movements are too elaborate to clearly describe here, and must be learned in class, from a qualified instructor.

Bokken #1

1-2 3-4 5-6 7-8 9-10 11-12 13 (silent) −

Bokken #2

1-2 3-4 5-6 7-8 9– 10– 11-12 13 (silent) –

Jo #1

1 ... 2– 3-4-5-6 7-8-9-10-11-12 – 13 14-15-16-17
18-19-20-21-22

Jo #2

1...2– 3-4-5-6 7-8-9-10 11-12-13-14-15
16-17-18-19-20-21-22

In addition to the *kata* listed above, the following *jo* exercises are for perfecting movement and voice. These exercises or drills are called *"Ki Okuri Undo* with *Jo,* which means "Ki Continuing Exercise with Jo." The regu-lar Jo moves are to be repeated as indicated by the numbers called out, without ceasing.

Jo #1

1 ... 2-1-2-3-4-5-6 3-4-5-6 3-4-5-6 7-8-9-10-11-
12 7-8-9-10-11-12 7-8-9-10-11-12-13 14-15-16– 13
14-15-16-17 14-15-16-17 18-19-20-21-22-1 18-19-
20-21-22 – 1

Jo #2

1...2— 1— 2— 3--4-5-6— 3--4-5-6 7-8-9-10 7-8-9-10 11-12-13-14 11-12-13-14-15 16-17-18-19-20-21-22-1-15 16-17-18-19-20-21-22-1

HIGH UPON HIGH

An old, retired swordsman said, "There are levels in the course of mastery throughout your life. At the lowest level of skill and ability, one thinks of himself and others as poor. He thinks this because he has mastered only a little. Needless to say, a person at this level is not at all useful.

At the middle level, one is still useless, but he can at least understand that he and others have mastered only a little.

At a high level, since a person has made something his own, he is proud of his accomplishments. And he is also glad at the praise of others. He grieves over the short-comings of others. This kind of person is at least useful.

At a higher level, one pretends to know nothing, yet others understand that he holds an upper hand. The majority of people cannot get beyond this level.

Beyond this higher level, there is one further step; THE LEVEL OF THE TRACKLESS ROAD. If you travel deeper into the trackless road, infinite secrets will finally appear.

Then you can never see the end of your mastery. Then you truly realize how lacking you are. You have only to go ahead with your intention of mastery in mind. You go forward without pride and without humility.

Yagyu Munemori Tajima no Kami (the Shogun's fencing instructor) once said, "I know nothing about how to win over others. I only know the way to win over myself."

Your life is something you build every day. You must convince yourself that you have surpassed yesterday, and tomorrow you must feel that you have surpassed today. In this way there is no end to your mastery.

Tsunemoto Yamamoto 1710

CHAPTER 13

ACTING AS *OTOMO*
TRAVELING WITH SENSEI

The word *"Otomo"* means "humble attendant." The duty of the *otomo* is to accompany the Sensei everywhere, to be at his side at all times, and to assist him in all his needs. It is an honor and privilege to be selected as *otomo,* and a task that is to be executed with great care and respect. However, in a general sense, the spirit of *otomo* is not simply a mantle that is taken on only at certain times, but an attitude to be made a part of your character. It is awareness training in its highest form. You must always be two steps ahead of the Sensei. If he has to ask you or tell you to do something, to remind you of something he needs, then you have failed in your obligation.

The following are a few specific examples to give an idea of the responsibilities of an *otomo:*

ACTING AS OTOMO

1. When picking up the Sensei, or meeting him some where, always arrive ahead of time. "On time" is always too late. Fifteen minutes to half an hour ahead of time is not too early. The world is made of change. Something always seems to "come up." Arriving early gives you time to adjust to a change, or solve a problem, so your ultimate responsibility is not compromised.

2. Check Sensei's equipment (traveling bag, gi bag, jo and ken bag) ahead of time to make sure nothing is missing, even if he says everything is there. Your job is to make sure he has everything he needs with him. It is not his fault, but <u>yours</u>, if something is missing.

3. All planning for transportation, traveling funds, tickets, arranging for reservations, flight schedules, etc. are your responsibility. Sensei should never have to make these arrangements him/herself.

4. Sensei is never to introduce himself to someone he is unfamiliar with. Your job is always to announce that he is coming, and to introduce him. Do not then introduce yourself, unless you are asked.

5. At public gatherings, such as meetings, parties or banquets, always make sure to take care of Sensei's needs first and foremost. Do not begin eating or drinking until he has been served and has begun.

6. The Sensei is never to be left alone. He must be accompanied at all times, unless he specifically

requests otherwise. Even then, he must not be far from your mind. You should be nearby and available, if there should be a change. You want to be with him until he retires to sleep, and then be thinking of what will be required when he awakens.

7. Before Sensei begins a class or seminar, make sure all of his equipment is in place where he will need it. Weapons, notes, drinking water, a bench or chair near by, and drawing board must all be in place. You must arrange ahead of time with the host, to be sure that these things will be provided, if you do not bring them with you. Never rely upon someone else, and <u>never</u> assume it will be taken care of.

8. Contact the host ahead of time, in order to satisfy yourself that all aspects of etiquette related to your Sensei are being taken into account. You must take care, at the same time, not to insult the host. Sometimes you must be creative in your work. But always your Sensei's needs are foremost.

9. During class, while Sensei is teaching, you must not slack your awareness and simply train like the other students. Changes will occur, needs will arise, and you must solve these before they become a problem.

10. After class, the Sensei's hakama must be folded, and your hakama must be folded. The Sensei may choose to stand around and talk with the students briefly, giving you some time to complete these tasks, or

he may depart for the dressing room immediately. This contingency must be arranged for ahead of time. Make sure that you have assigned assistants to take care of the hakamas, and other aspects of his equipment, while you are helping him change clothes. Often, the Sensei is leaving quickly, to go to dinner or elsewhere. All training clothes and equipment must be properly cared for in a short period of time. As an example, if his gi is wet, it must be hung up to dry. At the same time, you must not leave the Sensei's side. Other things will arise. You will need to be discussing with the host about the evenings arrangements. It is your responsibility to recruit all help necessary to leave nothing un-done, and in a timely manner.

11. Do not imagine that, since you, as otomo, travel with the Sensei and know his or her teaching well, you have the authority to give advice or direction to other students or instructors during your functioning as otomo. You do not. Your attention must be completely dedicated to your task at hand, which is providing space for the teacher to focus exclusively on his or her teaching responsibilities.

In summary, I repeat that acting as otomo is awareness training. Awareness of everyone and all things within your sphere of responsibility, at all times. We are used to thinking only of our own personal needs. This is not wrong, but simply very ineffective. We cannot be thinking only of ourselves, and at the same time effectively take care of the needs of others. The Sensei must be free to concentrate on teaching those around him. If he is distracted by your inefficiency, he cannot do that. Remember, nothing is too small or too big to be considered outside of your range of responsibility. A high-ranking Sensei recently remarked, "Otomo is very easy. There is no mystery; only one thing to remember. Just put your Master in as high a position as you can conceive of, and put yourself completely in his shadow."

CHAPTER 14

THE *KI IRE KI BARAI* PRAYER

The *Ki Ire Ki Barai prayer* is not commonly utilized by Aikidoists. However, Suzuki Sensei had a deep appreciation of this prayer, as taught by Koichi Tohei Sensei, and practiced it regularly. As Tohei Sensei taught this to us, it is to be used in two basic ways. First, we use Ki Ire Ki Barai as a kind of ceremonial prayer when blessing a dojo, a new building, or a piece of land, or as described below. Second, we can use Ki Ire Ki Barai as a daily prayer. We use this as a part of the Omiki ceremonies for the beginning and end of the training year, as well as a daily kind of affirmation and prayer of gratitude.

The first part of the prayer is Ki Ire. Ki Ire is made up of repaeating three times the phrase, "*Shinpo uchu rei kanno soku genjo*," which means "Blessed Universal Spirit, in this present moment may I directly experience your Presence." This tends to encourage a unified state of mind for everyone present.

The second part of this prayer, Ki Barai, is performed as described below. The purpose of this part of the prayer is to cut all suffering. Ki Barai is the cutting of *"Ku"* or *"Kurushii,"* which means "suffering." Suffering, struggle, or distress, comes about within each of us, in reaction to the pain of life's difficulties.

This entire, two-part prayer can be useful when traveling, meeting certain people, or going into any situation that might prove difficult, challenging, or disturbing. With Ki Ire we engender a positive feeling of well being, and with Ki Barai we discourage any kind of rejection or clinging in the moment, which we call suffering.

It is important to remember that this is never to be done with the intention to control anyone or alter any situation. This is always to be done above the head of the person, or over the top of the building, road, etc. It is never done directly into another person or thing. When we perform this ceremony, we are supporting the clarity of our own state of mind, not attempting to cause others to alter theirs. We desire only to support, or help people, family, friends, students, the community, or the country. As with everything in Life, it is as effective as your faith is deep.

The following shows technically how to perform Ki Ire and K Barai. However, if you are not already familiar with this action, you should learn this directly from a knowledgeable instructor.

The Ki Ire Ki Barai Prayer

1. Stand facing the *shomen* if in the dojo, holding your hands, at eye height, in a position of prayer, palm to palm.

2. Repeat three times: *"Shinpo uchu rei kanno soku genjo."* The first two times are the same, spoken at an even pitch and tempo. The third time they are spoken with a decending pitch and a slower tempo.

3. Turn to face away from the Shomen. Fold hands three times in the following way: The firstime, fold hands together as in *toitsu no in,* with the exception that the *middle* fingers are extended, and the right thumb is folded over the left. The second time, fold in the standard *toitsu no in* position, with the *first* fingers extended and the *left* thumb over the right. The third time is the same as the first. At each of these positions execute a verbal *Kiai,* very loudly, sounding like *"ee-yay-ee."*

4. Holding the first finger of the right hand slightly over lapped over the second finger, and extending both, cut the air first diagonally down from right to left, then from the finish point of the first cut, diagonally down from left to right, then cut straight down intersecting both previous cuts. At each of these cuts, execute the same *Kiai,* again very loudly.

5. When blessing a building or a general area, items number 3 and 4 can be repeated in four directions; East, South, West and North, always clockwise. (In dojo begin always at *shomen).*

CHAPTER 15

TRAINING WITH WATER

There are two additional forms of Aikido training that are less commonly known. They are as follows:

SENSHIN NO GYO

Senshin no Gyo is basically early morning splashing of oneself with very cold water. The purpose of this training is to cleanse the mind or to make the mind positive. If we bring any negative thoughts into the new day, either from the previous day, or from a troubled sleep, the mind can be cleansed through this treatment. In addition, one might say that after an early morning dousing with icy water, any difficulty the subsequent day offers may be viewed with relative ease. This promotes positive thinking.

Senshin no gyo can be practiced anywhere there is a body of water, or even a bucket. A garden hose can be used to fill the bucket, though it is much easier, (and not so long a wait in between splashes), if a tub is available to dip into. Taking a cold shower is often used as a substitute, but a constant stream of water is somewhat less effective.

RIVER *MISOGI*

"River" *Misogi* is a somewhat more severe form of cold-water training. This discipline involves immersing the entire body in a river, pond, lake, or the ocean, in winter. Usually this is done once a year, between January 1st and 3rd. The purpose of this training is very similar to Sen shin no gyo, except that the idea is to clear away any remnants from the entire previous year, and prepare oneself for the New Year.

In Japan, in the old days, Koichi Tohei Sensei would lead the group to a nearby river, the waters of which flow directly from the distant snow covered mountains. All were clad in bathing attire, and perhaps zori to protect the feet. Tohei Sensei would lead the group in some Aiki taiso to get the blood moving. Tohei Sensei would then perform Ki Ire Ki Barai, and all in the group would utter a loud kiai. Then everyone would descend into the icy waters, submerging up to the chest or more.

Immediately following this early morning dunking, the entire group would return to the dojo for an hour or more of Soku Shin no Gyo, or "bell" misogi.

This discipline is practiced by many Aikido groups throughout the world. Almost always a source of cold water can be found in January. Here in Hawaii, however, where winter air and water temperatures are in the seventies, water dunking is a hardly a sacrifice. So we must travel to Japan or elsewhere for a real "river" misogi.

In 1961, Morihei Ueshiba Sensei, visited Maui and performed a formal blessing for our dojo. He brushed the above calligraphy, "Ai-Ki-Do", and presented it to Suzuki Sensei. It now hangs on our dojo wall.

CHAPTER 16

THE LIVING PRINCIPLES

The following is a listing of various "Principles" formulated by Tohei Sensei:

FIVE PRINCIPLES OF ONE POINT

1. A posture in which you do not focus on the lower abdomen.
2. A posture in which the upper body weight falls on the One Point.
3. A posture in which you don't notice your breath.
4. A posture in which you can accept all things.
5. A posture that initiates all action.

FIVE PRINCIPLES OF RELAXATION

1. A posture in which you can settle the power of the whole body naturally.
2. A posture in which you relax your body without losing power.

3. A posture in which you appear bigger than you are.
4. A posture in which you are the strongest.
5. A posture of non-dissension.

FIVE PRINCIPLES OF WEIGHT UNDERSIDE

1. A posture which is most comfortable.
2. A posture in which your body feels light.
3. A posture in which your Ki is fully extended.
4. A flexible posture in which you can adapt to changing circumstances.
5. A posture in which you can see and feel things clearly.

FIVE PRINCIPLES OF EXTENDING KI

1. A posture in which you do not pay attention to your body.
2. A posture in which centrifugal force is working.
3. A posture with merciful eyes and a kind face.
4. A posture which is quiet.
5. A posture in which you are positive and accept all things.

FIVE PRINCIPLES OF KI MEDITATION

1. A posture of holding.
2. A posture of letting go.

3. A posture of harmony.
4. A posture in which you can feel the creation of the universe.
5. A posture in which you can feel the movement of Ki of the universe.

FIVE PRINCIPLES OF KI EXERCISE

1. A posture in which the one point in the lower abdomen is the center.
2. A posture of extending Ki.
3. A posture in which you can relax and feel free.
4. A posture in which there is no tension.
5. A posture in which you can feel the rhythm.

FIVE PRINCIPLES OF KI BREATHING

1. Exhale gradually with ease.
2. Exhale with the smallest sound possible.
3. Exhale gradually from head to toe.
4. Inhale through the tip of the nose and fill the body from toe to head.
5. After inhaling, calm yourself at the one point in the lower abdomen.

FIVE PRINCIPLES OF KIATSU RYOHO

1. Extend Ki from the one point in the lower abdomen.
2. Do not stop the flow of Ki.
3. Press perpendicularly towards the center of the body.
4. Concentrate infinitely small at the finger tips.
5. Be aware of the flow, and not the points.

FIVE PRINCIPLES OF KI TEST

1. It is a test to check state of mind not state of body.
2. Teach others based on their level of development.
3. Test others to support them, not to make them fail.
4. Understand Ki Principles through testing others.
5. The teaching is the moon, not the finger pointing to the moon.

FIVE PRINCIPLES OF SHINSHIN TOITSU AIKIDO

1. Ki is extending
2. Know your partner's mind
3. Respect your partner's Ki
4. Put yourself in the place of your partner.
5. Lead and move

FIVE PRINCIPLES OF KEN WITH KI

1. Hold the bokken lightly.
2. The tip of a bokken must be calm.

3. Use the weight of a bokken.
4. Do not lose your attention.
5. Mind moves first.

FIVE PRINCIPLES OF JO WITH KI

1. Hold the jo lightly.
2. Hold with the hand closest to your body.
3. Move the jo freely.
4. Always keep one hand on a jo when moving.
5. The line drawn by the tip of jo is never broken.

FIVE PRINCIPLES OF INSTRUCTING

1. Have the spirit to encourage success for yourself and others.
2. Be humble.
3. Teach virtue, not strength.
4. Teach everyone equally.
5. Be positive.

FIVE PRINCIPLES OF LEARNING

1. Be open.
2. Continue your study without becoming bored.
3. Practice daily.
4. Change your subconscious mind.
5. Have the mind of an instructor.

FIVE PRINCIPLES OF SETSUDO

1. Follow the way of the universe.
2. Do not use the way of the universe for personal benefit.
3. Practice what you teach.
4. Share according to the level of the person.
5. Have a mind to progress together.

FIVE PRINCIPLES OF EDUCATING CHILDREN

1. Let children have fun while learning.
2. Never let them get injured.
3. Recognize all progress and acknowledge with positive words.
4. Set boundaries clearly.
5. Have a positive mind when you correct them.

FIVE PRINCIPLES OF SLEEPING

1. Unify mind and body.
2. Understand that mind moves body.
3. Allow the blood to flow freely to the legs and feet.
4. Let the brain be calm.
5. Have a cool head and warm feet.

FIVE PRINCIPLES OF OFFICE WORK

1. Don't wait to be told what to do.
2. Take notes for everything.
3. Don't postpone what you can do now.
4. Plan for tomorrow before you go to bed tonight.
5. Clean up after working.

FIVE PRINCIPLES OF SALES

1. Understand the value of the product.
2. Be positive.
3. See that the product benefits the customer, instead of begging them to buy it.
4. Always follow up after sales.
5. Leave a positive impression with the customer, even if you could not sell the product.

FIVE PRINCIPLES OF MANAGEMENT

1. First, be positive.
2. Forget personal benefit, and work to benefit others.
3. Practice calmness and be aware of the trends in your business.
4. Train people with the idea that they are the future of the business.
5. Have a mind to return profits to your community.

CHAPTER 17

THE MEANING OF AIKIDO

合 – **Ai**

氣 – **Ki**

道 – **Do**

合 – **Ai:** Most everyone commonly interprets Ai to mean "harmony." The calligraphy for this word Ai is made up of three separate characters, and literally means human, one, and mouth. So Ai means "human with one mouth." Maybe you can imagine the meaning already. What do we do with our mouth? We speak, we chant, we sing. So we can say that Ai means "everyone singing with one voice." "Harmony" is a good word to use for that. It is a popular one. But sometimes words have different meanings for different people. So it is important to look carefully at the source of important words like this. Of course, all kanji (Japanese calligraphy) originally came to Japan from ancient China. So this is Chinese from long ago. It is important to remember that when we look at these. So this is all people singing, or speaking with one voice; all humans unified.

The challenge with the word "harmony" is that we often conceive of harmony as two or more things coming together. However, this is a relative and limited view. Harmony, as it is used in the word Aikido, doesn't mean multiple things coming together. Harmony here means all things are already together, even though we might not perceive them as being in that condition. Humans are already one, unified. There is no need to make them one. We humans, through our limited and relative perception, actually make them separate. The way we see the world, and hence the way we see each other, is almost always relative, limited to time and space dimensions, you over there and me over here. So he definitely seems different and separate from me, and either better or worse off, but never the same.

Since we perceive this incredible variety, where everyone is apparently so different, then we must practice remembering that there is some fundamental essence that is one. And what is that? That is the question. If we are going to practice Ai, then we have to have some kind of deep contact with what that is, if that something can even be spoken, or defined. Maybe, when we speak it, or define it, it suddenly becomes part of that relative condition, and it is not what we meant to point to at all.

氣 – **Ki:** Ki is made up of two separate characters, and each has its own meaning, as with Ai. For the first character, on the top and to the right, we can say "clouds and rain", which would be coming down from the heavens. Or at the same time it can mean "steam", which would be rising up. And the symbol in the center, the second one, is the symbol for "rice." If this above is clouds and rain, then the rice is considered to be growing. If the first symbol is seen as steam, then the rice is cooking. In both cases, it is exploding outward. It is important to understand why they made these symbols to signify Ki of the universe. Obviously, to the ancient Chinese, the word Ki was very significant for them. Because if the rain didn't come and the rice crop didn't come in, they didn't live. They couldn't go to the grocery store and buy some more rice. If the crop didn't come in that year, there was a famine. Everyone suffered. So, having the rains come, having the rice crop be successful, and having the rice to eat as food, for the ancient Chinese this meant life itself. Therefore they used this combination of two symbols to represent Ki — life itself. Life.

道 — **Do:** Again, Do is made up of two symbols. The first one means "way". And this second one means "leader," or you can say "individual," or it also can even mean "prominence." So, we might say "the prominent way" or "the way of the prominent individual." So, yes, this is "Do", and most know that "Do" means "the way." Ju-do, Karate-do, Ken-do, Kyu-do, Aiki-do.

This is also made up of two symbols, which is telling us that there is a further qualification to the word "way." We have "leader", or "individual," added on to, or coupled with "way." What that is pointing to, or qualifying here, is that, yes, there is only one way, but that you have to come upon it from your particular individually conditioned mind. We can say that the action path through life of each individual person is unique. There is one general "way," but this "way" manifests in each of us uniquely. The way is not something that we must follow blindly. Our task it to awaken to the realization of that way, as it evolves in each of us.

Another note about this word: just about everyone has heard the word "tao" these days. This is "the way." But again, when we read or hear about the Taoist philosophy, we often interpret it as a sort of generalized way that everybody has to follow. And indeed it is, but you can only come upon it in a very individualistic and private way. You have to lead yourself to it. The way is the most prominent aspect of your character, at any given moment. The way is working itself out in you right now, at this instant. At every moment, that is what is happening in your life.

So maybe you can see why this practice was originally called "Aikido." These are very powerful symbols with huge implications. And realize that this word is meant to represent the potential that may be experienced. This is not an understanding, exactly, but more like a way of being. Hence the word "way."

Lets go back to Ki for a moment. We said the word "Ki" basically means "Life." Many people think Ki, Chi, Prana, Mana, etc. are some form of energy. This is not wrong. But people conceive of energy as a kind of a force, as in, "I can extend my Ki to you." Waaa!

But let's look a little closer. Our bodies are made of organs, our organs are made of cells, our cells are made of mole-cules, our molecules are made of atoms, atoms are made of subatomic particles, quarks, and so forth on down to the infinitely small. This can be seen, but of course only to a point. The problem begins when the things get smaller and smaller and smaller and "things" turn out to be not necessarily things. We think of a thing as an object, something substantial, matter. However, when the "thing" gets small enough, how you look for it dictates what it is when you find it. If you look at it a certain way, then it appears as matter, a particle. If you look at it in another way, then it appears as energy, a wave. What we see is what the structure of this universe is comprised of. Which one? Well, one or the other, depending upon what you are looking for! You get a kind of Yogi Berra answer here. "When you come to a fork in a road, take it."

If we ask, "Is it that or is it this?", the answer is "yes." And this is not the same as saying it's "both." The answer to the question is "yes." So, we find that the "essence" of this universal structure is not so easy to pin down and define, particularly when we look very closely at it.

THE MEANING OF AIKIDO

Koichi Tohei Sensei said very simply, when we look closer and closer, that tiniest, infinitely small fundamental building block of life, is Ki. This "Ki" is the fundamental structure of what we call life. Whether it goes together to make a boulder, a racing stream, or human being, it doesn't matter. You can take an atom out of a lizard's tale and stick it in your brain and your brain won't know the difference. It doesn't matter, on that fundamental level. Of course, once it gets manifested and organized more, then of course it begins to make a difference. You can't take an organ out of a lizard and put it in your body. Naturally, it doesn't work that way.

So... at a fundamental level, all life is one; undifferentiated. Not one "thing", now...we can't say one "thing." We are not able to say this is either a "thing" (particle) or an "energy" (wave). We can say that it is one, meaning universally the same, in that it is completely interchangeable. And don't forget, it is what we are made of, nothing else. And we can also say that it exists now, because it can only be perceived in the present, and so, for us, only exists here and now. It's what this is right here. So in this sense, we can say that Life (Ki) is universal (everywhere the same) and present (always only now).

So...we can say that Ki equals Universal Presence.

GLOSSARY OF TERMS

The following is a list of Japanese terms which you will often hear used in your training. It is essential that you study and learn these terms, not only for practical reasons, but also to help you discover the many aspects of Aikido training.

Agura   sitting cross-legged.

Aikido
  -Ai   Harmony, union with, oneness.

  -Ki   The essential Life Force, the funda-
                   mental creative energy.

  - Do   The Way or Path.

Ani-deshi   Senior disciple.

Atemi   Striking or hitting vital points.

Atotori   "He who comes after" — he or she who
                   is selected to be the next leader of a
                   dojo or group.

Bokken/Bokuto   Wooden training sword.

Budo
  -Bu   Military, martial.

  -Do   The Way or Path

Budoka   Student of Budo

Bushido   The ways which fighting nobles,
                   knights, samurai should observe intheir
                   life as well as their vocation. The
                   precepts of knighthood. Code of moral
                   principals which the samurai were
                   required to observe.

Chikara   Strength

Chudan   Middle level; area from waist to neck.

Dai   Large

Dai Sensei   Great teacher

Dan   Black belt rank. There are ten stations
                   of Dan, as follows:
                   Shodan – 1stdan
                   Nidan – 2nd dan
                   Sandan – 3rd dan
                   Yondan – 4th dan
                   Godan – 5thdan
                   Rokudan – 6thdan
                   Nanadan – 7th dan

Hachidan — 8th dan
Kyudan — 9th dan
Judan — 10th dan

Deshi	Disciple of a certain skilled practitioner, not necessarily martial art. Not the same as "student." "Student" means you are studying with someone for a certain period of time, as in school, or college, during the day time. "Deshi" means you are obligated to the teacher, for life.
Do	Torso; area from waist to shoulders. Also, the way.
Dojo	The training hall. The place where the way to harmony with fundamental life force (Ki) is practiced.
Enshin ryoku	Centrifugal force of a technique.
Fudoshin	Immovable mind.
Fudotai	Immovable body.
Gedan	Lower level; below the waist.
Genkan	Front entrance of dojo.

Gi	Training uniform — usually white muslin material. The padded type is best for beginners.
Hajime	Begin.
Hakama	A black (sometimes dark blue) split pleated skirt/pants worn over the *gi*. Only *shodan* rank (1st degree black belt) and above are permitted to wear the hakama. In some dojos, women of lesser rank than *shodan* are permitted to wear.
Hanmi	The triangular stance. This position is meant to be relaxed, comfortable, and natural, and should in no way look or feel artificial or stiff. From the correct *hanmi* position, one can move readily in any direction.

ai hanmi — *nage* and *uke* have same foot forward.

gyaku hanmi-nage and *uke* have opposite foot forward.

Hanmi Handachi	Techniques where *nage* is sitting and *uke* is standing.
Hantai	Opposite
Happo giri	Cutting the sword in eight directions of the compass.

Hara	The entire lower abdominal area — not to be confused with "one point in the lower abdomen."
Hidari	Left side.
Hombu	Head office of an organization.
Irimi	Moving to the inside, or moving into.
Jo	Wooden training staff. The approximate correct length is indicated by the distance between the palms of one's outstretched hands.
Kagura	In *Misogi,* the two persons that assist, seated opposite to the *Osa.*
Kamae	Posture or position
Kagami Biraki	Japanese new years celebration. It is usually a major dojo event with special classes and a lecture by the Chief Instructor. It is traditionally celebrated on the first Sunday in January.
Kan	Intuition.
Kata	A formal, prearranged exercise.
Katana	The long sword worn by the Japanese samurai.

Kesagiri   Cutting with the sword diagonally from shoulder to hip.

Keiko   Practice session, training.

Kiai   Literally "a meeting of the spirits," this is a penetrating cry or scream originating in the *Hara*. In Aikido, the standard form of *Kiai is* "ee-yay-ee"

Kime   Focus of physical and/or mental energy.

Ki musubi   To tie the ki together; to move as one.

Ki nagare   Energy flow.

Kohai   A student or teacher who is the same rank as you, but began training after you, is your *kohai*.

Kokoro   Spirit, heart, will.

Kokyu   Literally "breath or breathing," this refers to the power generated through extensive *ki* breathing and emanating from the one point in the lower abdomen.

Kokyuho	Calmness breathing practice as taught by Koichi Tohei Sensei.
Kyu	Ranks prior to *Shodan:*

Mudansha (non-ranked student)

Adults:
5th *kyu* — blue belt
4th *kyu* — purple belt
3rd *kyu* — purple belt
2nd *kyu* — brown belt
1 st *kyu* — brown belt

Children:
10th kyu — white belt
9th *kyu* — green belt
8th *kyu* — orange belt
7th *kyu* — orange belt
6th *kyu* — blue belt

Maai	"Harmonious relationship" The correct distance to be maintained between opponents. The immediate surroundings, and one's own position determine this spacing.
Mae	In front.
Migi	Right side.

Misogi	Generally, the act of purifying mind and body. Specifically, a side-training discipline in Shinshin Toitsu Aikido known as *Soku Shin no Gyo.* (See section on *"Misogi"*).
Nage	A throw, one who throws, or executes a technique.
Nanadan	Seventh dan or level of rank. Never say "Shichidan" as "shichi" is a homonym for "death." Similarly, we never say "Shidan" for Fourth Dan. We say "Yondan."
Osa	The instructor who leads *Misogi,* seated to the right of the Shomen.
O *Sensei*	Great, or original teacher. In *Aikido* refers to *Morihei Ueshiba,* the founder of modern *Aikido.*
Otomo	*Tomo* means attendant, or especially traveling attendant. O, when attached to the front of a word in Japanese, means "a humbling of self." So *otomo* means a particularly humble attendant.
Randori	A single n*age* against multiple attackers, usually employing limited types of attack.

Rei	Bow, the command to bow.
Reiseishin	The Spirit that is One with the Spirit of the Universe.
Sabaki	Body motion.
Samurai	One who follows the Way. A warrior, knight; one charged with the protection of society. See *"budo, bushido."*
Sempai	A student or teacher who is the same rank as you, but began training before you did, is your *sempai*.
Sensei	Teacher. One who gives instruction. More importantly, one who leads the way.
Sensen no sen	Seizing the initiative just as the opponent thinks to attack.
Shiho	Four directions.
Shikko	Moving from a kneeling position. Also called *"samurai* walk."
Shin	Mind, spirit, heart.

Shinken shobu   Life and death training or experience.

Shomen   The honored symbol of *Ki* and picture of the Master mounted in the center front of the training area.

Shokushu   A brief, uplifting statement used prior to training. *Tohei Sensei* has composed twenty-two of these sayings which are read and repeated phrase by phrase before each class. Used to center oneself, prepare oneself for training.

Shoshin   A beginners mind.

Shunshinkan   The name of the Maui Ki-Aikido main dojo, which is the Hawaii Ki Federation hombu dojo, presented by Tohei Sensei. *Shun* = leader; *shin* = mind, *kan* = building.

Sokuboku   *Soku* = breath; *boku* = wood. The wooden clappers used to signify the changes in breathing and meditation.

Suburi   Repetitive bokken exercises developing basic techniques of motion and cutting.

Suki   A momentary gap in concentration allowing an opening to be attacked.

Suihei	Horizontal
Suwariwaza	Techniques requiring the *nage* and *uke* to perform from the kneeling position.
Tai	Body, form, sometimes style. Also used as Kiai during meditation sessions.
Taigi	Body art, technique.
Tanto/tanken	Wooden training knife. All wooden training weapons are to be treated as if they were sharp steel. That is, if one can successfully view the wooden weapon as steel, then when faced suddenly with steel, one can view the steel as wood.
Tenkan	Turning outside or away in a circular motion to dissipate an oncoming force.
Uke	One who is thrown; one who follows.
Ukemi	The art of falling without injury. It is said that one's ability to throw is only as good as one's ability to fall.
Uchideshi	Literally "inside student" — a student that lives, works, and trains, at the Headquarters or dojo.
Waza	Technique or system of techniques.

GLOSSARY OF TERMS

Yudansha	Those who hold the rank of *Shodan* and above.
Zagi handachi	Techniques performed with one uke standing and nage sitting seiza.
Zarei	A seated bow
Zazen	Seated meditation, as in Zen Buddhist practice.
Zen	A Japanese school of Buddhism that advocates seated meditation as a means of attaining *satori*, the realization of non-separation from Universe.
Zengo	Front and back.
Zengo waza	Moving to the front and rear
Zenpo	Forward.
Zenpo Kaiten	A forward roll.
Zenshin	The entire mind/body/being
Zori	Sandals.

INTENSIVE TRAINING

Intensive training has a purpose. It is a time for concentrating on mastery; of one's mind, of one's body, of one's will.

In intensive training every martial art student has the opportunity to fulfill this purpose. However, whether the student seizes the opportunity and explores it in depth, or jilts it for life's leisures and pleasures depends on his or her <u>attitude</u> toward training.

The person who sincerely wants or understands "Life with Purpose" approaches the training with seriousness matching the intensity of a stalking tiger. The less sincere train ignorantly and often skimpily, perhaps led astray by false reason — to develop better health, carve a larger physique, to impress others, or attain a black belt. To assure proper development these persons must quickly realize a given purpose: They must at minimum demand best effort of themselves or fall prey to easy disappointments, for at this dojo, best effort is <u>expected</u>, not nurtured.

Those who reject the way of best effort may become the metaphorical "mosquito pupils" of Sensei's lectures. These are students who only appear during certain opportune seasons, or who arrive to savor the fluid wisdoms of distinguished guest teachers, then vanish until the next rain of benefits. And what of the "tea-kettle students" whose will to train remains lukewarm because they are externally motivated by ego needs. And too, the ones caught between the gears – wanting to train to a boil, but stopped by a needy spouse or fighting children. There are many among all these students who would feel more fulfilled elsewhere and indeed many do leave this dojo. Rare are the individuals who can steadily and intensely pursue their training year after year.

A 16th century samurai considered 10 years of intensive training not too long a period for reaching even a shallow realization. However, it is an occasional hermit or dedicated monk among us today who can afford to dedicate 10 years of life to training. Most of us must daily juggle time demands of education, family, employment, leisure and intensive training. Herein lies the problem even after the student has overcome his commitment excuses. "I've decided to train with the intensity of the tiger but how can I match the Ki level of a 10-year training period in my twice-a-week, interrupted classes?" Now the value of intensive training becomes apparent. Here is the opportunity for wholehearted, straining effort of the kind that will reap meaningful realization within this lifetime.

For those determined not to recycle through the garbage heap of lives, your frame of mind need only be as Sensei exhorts: "Take care of your other needs when you must, and stay home. But come to every class that you can. When you are in class, only train. Train intensely. Train seriously."

Unknown

WEBSITE:

www.curtissensei.com

www.mauiaikido.com

YOUTUBE:

Maui Ki Aikido:

Weapons videos

Tying Belt

Tying Hakama

Folding Hakama

Masa Katsu calligraphy

ABOUT THE AUTHOR

Christopher Curtis Sensei (Hachidan, Okuden, Lecturer, and Special Examiner)

Head Instructor – Maui Ki Aikido

Chief Instructor - Hawaii Ki Federation

Ki Society Advisor – Europe Ki Federation

Curtis Sensei's first encounter with Aikido was in 1968, with then student of Koichi Tohei Sensei, Yoshimitsu Yamada Sensei, in New York City. After attending a three-year meditation retreat, Curtis Sensei began training with his teachers Koichi Tohei Sensei (Japan) and Shinichi Suzuki Sensei (Maui) in 1974. Curtis Sensei served as Suzuki Sensei's otomo for many years, accompanying him as he traveled to attend and teach seminars in Japan, the United States, South America, and Europe.

Curtis Sensei now teaches regularly at Maui Ki-Aikido, and continues to travel and teach Aikido and Ki Principles in Europe, Russia, the United States, and throughout Hawaii. In 2004, Curtis Sensei was appointed as the official Ki Society representative for the Ki Society groups training in Europe, and in 2018 the Europe Ki Federation was established, bringing all Ki Society dojo in Europe together as one.

He has authored another book on Aikido, addressing the practice of Ki-Aikido in daily life, called "Letting Go."

CPSIA information can be obtained
at www.ICGtesting.com
Printed in the USA
LVHW042331200322
713959LV00001B/129